The Studio Within
collected writings
by Ted Katz

www.tedkatz.com
Portland, Oregon

Acknowledgments

Simply put, there would be no book without the critical contributions of Suzy Vitello, Phil Joslin, Wanda Gray, Brenda Johnson and Michael Labogin. I am indebted to each of you for your role in the creation of The Studio Within.

FOR MOM

Early in my life, after I'd had a painful disappointment, Mom cornered me in her kitchen.

"Sit down. We need to talk."

"It's late, Mom, and I'm tired. Tomorrow."

"*Now.* I hear bitterness in you and I'm not gonna have it. What's bothering you, Ted?"

So we faced one another across a table and talked through the night. *There will be no bitterness.*

The years passed, and one day Mom said to me, "You've had an interesting life, Ted - and some rough sea."

"I didn't think you knew about a lot of it."

"I know enough. A mother *feels* her children - she doesn't need details."

"Well what did you do about those feelings?"

"I went behind a door and cried; then I came back out again. No one needed to see me cry."

"But you never *said* much."

"What good would it have done? You needed to be you."

"I'll make a little book of stories for you, so you will *know* better."

"I would like that."

THE STUDIO WITHIN

Contents

PROLOGUE

"It has been said that writing comes more easily if you have something to say." - Sholom Asch

NO GAME OF SOLITAIRE

"Good Morning, Ted."

"How's the coffee?"

It's still dark outside as I come into the studio but they're already up and at it.

"Hey Ted, here's a story for you!"

"Remember when we stood in the park and got rained on?"

"You wanted that dog but Mom didn't!"

"Can one of you open a window in here."

I'd been dreading coming to the studio *to write* because I didn't know what to say, or how to get started. So I spent time hanging around, thinking about this and that, and waiting for something to happen. Friends would ask, "Did you write today?" "Kind of," I would tell them. But the years of letters and photographs I'd counted on to get me going smelled like dead leaves and I didn't know how to wake them up again. I was thinking about throwing them out, and then one day they started talking - called themselves *histories*, and said they had nowhere else to go.

9

After lying around for years in boxes and albums, they started coming to life when I began telling about them, telling me back what they remembered differently.

"I never talked like that, Ted. And I didn't say that, either!"

So, for me, writing has been no game of solitaire - the *histories* are all over the studio, talking to each other. Some simply sit there all day talking to themselves. They must be glad to get out of their boxes, and I let them be.

"I'm glad to get out of that box, lying under them! I never liked them anyway."

When the *histories* get too excited - and they can - I ask them to settle down so I can work. But when I get lost in a story, the *histories* help me find my way.

"Hey, wait a minute — that's not what went on!"

Some voices from longest ago are only thin threads of sound - maybe because they've traveled so far.

"Mom wouldn't have said it like that."

Best sometimes, to just sit in the studio, let the histories chatter - and listen. And sometimes, I can't hear them but can only feel them. So on those days, I sit and feel. Nothing wrong with that *but when they talk, I listen* - and write it down. If one won't talk, there's no story; if one will, there is. As I said, there's nothing solitary, for me, about writing.

"It's my turn!"

"Listen to this!"

A massage therapist once told me, "A bad massage is when I can count the strokes. There's no touch." I guess writing could be like that – when letters on a page are not heartbeats, a story might have no *touch*. Then, *histories* - out of the boxes with your anger, laughter, pain and love - talk to me. Alone in here? Not on *your* lives.

GROWING UP

"Everything has a beginning." - Kiowa

SAVING ETHEL FOGELMAN

Every summer in August, we went to the countryside for a week. The year I turned ten, Mom's friend, Ethel Fogelman, came to stay with us on a dairy farm. I thought Ethel was very glamorous because she had bright red lips and long yellow hair that she twisted all over her head. I wished my mother would do something like that. Ethel looked like a movie star. Sometimes she would spend a long time in her cabin with the curtains drawn. Mom said she was taking care of her roots, which sounded like magic. I thought Ethel was really something.

Anyway, I used to hang out a lot at the swimming hole, which was just a big pond with a log floating in the middle. You had to wade in by walking on pillowy mud, which was icky at first, and then felt good. I caught tadpoles in that pond, and you could feel them batting into your legs when you tip-toed out to deep water.

Well one afternoon, Ethel came for a swim. She coiled that yellow hair up on top of her head and entered the pond like a Viking ship paddling out to join me in the water, holding her head high. I had never seen anything like it. There was Ethel, splendid vessel, beside me, going for the log. And she was doing just fine until I told her to keep going because her feet could no longer touch the bottom where we were. Well, then what? Down she went like an anchor. Her hair unwound and spreads across the water like yellow seaweed. There I was, doggy-paddling in place

15

thinking that's really pretty, and waiting for her to come back up.

Then I remember that stuff is attached to Ethel, and she's been down there for some time - maybe checking out her roots. I better go down and see what's what. Ethel doesn't look too good, so I pull her up and haul her out to the log - and toss her on top. And I'm thinking, *she goes down shining and comes up with her lights out.* Her hair doesn't look so great either. She's hanging on that log, looking like a wet cheeseburger, and I'm wanting to drop her back in the water except Mom is jumping up and down on the tadpoles, hollering, "Pull 'er out!' Mom must have run into the pond without her glasses or she would see that Ethel is spread on the log.

I don't find out 'til supper that she was drowning down there, not checking out her roots. It didn't matter. Ethel wasn't glamorous anymore. That pond water put out her star. Some things don't look good wet. And anyway, movie stars don't drown.

GOLDEN GELDING

"Do you remember that little strip of park where Broad Street and York Road come together? There were benches there. I used to sit there and you would run into the street. Who was gonna see you? They couldn't see you because you were running so fast. I tied a rope around you and held on to the other end. You were a good baby until you started to run. Then you were a little boy."

For a long time, I liked to pretend I was a horse. I had a lot of hair and I liked to run and shake it. I think it made me feel free. Once I thought about being a lion but I didn't do it. I like the way horses run better. Anyway, I galloped everywhere. Mom says she used to tie a rope around me to hold on to me. Mom's friend, Ethel, took her boy to a child psychiatrist when he thought he was a hamster. Ethel told Mom the man was good, so Mom took me to see him, and he told her I had imagination and she should take me home.

I asked Mom what imagination was and she said, "That's enough!"

So I looked at lots of pictures of horses and decided to be a golden gelding because the name sounded nice. No one set me straight about that until years later, talking to a farmer, I found out about geldings. But I still think it sounds good.

Mom and Gram decided that horses, as well as kids, should have culture and that meant learning to play the piano. And that's how I came to Miss Frankel. Ethel told Mom about her, so Mom figured she was good. It turned out for me she was better than good - until the end. But that comes later.

So I would get off of the bus and trot over to Miss Frankel's and stand there, neighing as loud as I could. Miss Frankel came to the door, whinnying back and we cantered together to the piano. If the lesson went well, Miss Frankel would trot into her kitchen and get me an apple. I played my heart out for Miss Frankel, and Mom and Gram thought she was terrific. I didn't tell them she was a horse.

But dark clouds began to gather over this pasture. One day, I came early for my lesson and, while waiting for another pupil to finish up, I found a little book on a shelf in the waiting room. It was called *Of Mice and Men*. I liked that a lot. It might be fun to be a mouse - but not a hamster, like Burton Fogelman. I wanted to read that book, and decided to just take it and bring it back next week. During my lesson, I played well, and when Miss Frankel went to get my apple, I slipped the book into my sheet music and took it home with the apple. I couldn't find anything interesting in that book about mice or men. The next week, I brought it back and told Miss Frankel that I had borrowed it and didn't like it. Miss Frankel got a little crazy and said, first, that I should have asked before I took it. Then, she said it was not a book for children, and that there were things in it that I shouldn't be reading about.

"What's wrong with mice?"

"It's not about mice."

"Then what's it about?"

"That's enough. And don't tell your parents that you found that book here."

"Why?"

"Because it's not a nice book."

That did it! I was going to get that book out of there again and find the bad stuff. So I played like an angel, and when Miss Frankel went to get my apple, I ran to the book shelf but she was a faster horse than I was. The book was gone, and it never came back but I found it in a bookstore, bought it, carried it home under my coat, and hid it in my room where I kept the other bad things. I looked through that book a lot and couldn't find the bad stuff. Years later, in a college lit course, I did.

Meanwhile, back at Miss Frankel's, the clouds are growing still darker. An incident occurs that will lead to the end of my piano lessons. I can still hear that fat girl playing Debussy's *Claire de Lune*. It happens one morning, when I arrive too early for my lesson, and hear this pretty sound coming from the room with the piano in it. Soon this girl about fourteen walks out of that room carrying more sheet music than I have. When it's my turn to be in that room, I see a piece of music lying on top of the piano. It has a yellow cover with little green leaves on it.

"Is that what she was playing?"

"Yes. It's lovely."

"Can I play it too?"

"Not yet."

"Why not?"

"Because you're not mature enough yet."

"How long will that take?"

"Soon enough. When you're a little older."

Well, two things happened then at the same time. One, being ten started to bother me. Two, I wanted to play that piece. Miss Frankel must have needed money because I told her I wanted to stop playing the piano, and walked out of there with *Claire de Lune*. The minute I got home, I went to our piano and kneaded maturity into those keys. I bent and swayed, pushed and pulled. It was sounding mature to me. How's *this*, Miss Frankel! Mature *enough*, Miss Frankel? Gram came and sat next to the piano and listened. I knew she would like just about anything I did, and swayed more.

"It's supposed to sound like moonlight," I told her.

"Sounds pretty good to me," she replied.

"Does it sound mature to you?"

"Pretty good."

So there.

But Miss Frankel had her limits. Neighing was okay; messing with music was not. The two dollars I brought each week didn't buy me maturity. Miss Frankel just put down her foot. And so did I. Things changed between us. We came apart over *Claire*, and one day I took my last piano lesson, and my apple, and galloped off to look for maturity somewhere else.

Today, I still shake my hair and whinny, although I gallop more slowly - and only when no one's looking. It seems that every time I sit still, trouble finds me. I still like the sound of golden gelding, and sometimes wonder if Bella Frankel would think I'm mature enough today to play *Claire de Lune* - or read her little book about men and mice.

BATTERED BRIDES

Mom's on the phone a lot. When she's not talking to Ethel Fogelman, she's firing at Henrietta. I don't know if Henrietta has a last name because all Mom ever says is, "If you ask me, Hen." So she's talking about Nora from Russia, who lives in our building, and she's saying, "If you ask me, Hen, she's got *airs*."

I never saw them, so I ask Mom, "What are *airs*, Mom?" and she says, "Just let it go." That means, "I'm not going to tell you." When I see Nora from Russia in our building, I look at her and see nothing. I wonder where she puts the *airs*.

Nora from Russia has a daughter, Ilene. Mom says Ilene is not from Russia. That's good. Nora's always going on about Ilene this and Ilene that. Like how she's gonna be a ballerina, like Cyd Charisse, which she didn't become. What she does do is marry an *attoorney*. There's another word I don't know, so I go out and buy a book called, How To Increase Your Vocabulary, but it doesn't have the words I'm looking for, like *airs* and *attorney* - or *battered*. Every time we go to Nora's apartment, she puts on a record called The Dance of the *Battered* Bride, and Ilene dances to it. *Not again! How many times do we have to watch this thing?* Ilene has nice legs. I wonder if *battered* brides get cooked - like pancakes. Ilene looks like a pancake. I mean she's kind of round with small eyes.

I ask Mom what a *battered* bride is, and she says it's a lady with *issues*. I wonder if *issues* are like *airs*.

Mom says, "That's enough."

So this time I look up *issues* in the dictionary and I think that Mom and Nora both have them. Mom and Nora could even be *battered* brides. But Ilene couldn't - maybe later, when she marries the *attoorney*. Meanwhile, Nora and Mom are always hugging each other in the elevator. Something's not right.

"If you ask me, Hen, she's getting worse."

More *airs*, I figure. Where does she keep the things? How come Mom sees them all the time and I don't? Then one day, Dad runs into Nora's husband on the elevator and says, "Ed, your wife's a pain in the ass."

Well, Nora finds out and wants for Dad to apologize. Mom tells Dad no way because Nora *is* a pain in the ass.

"That's not a nice thing for Dad to say, Mom," I tell her.

"Well, she's a pain in the ass, that's all, and your father's not apologizing."

Five minutes later, I hear her on the phone, "She had it coming, Hen."

So what do *I* think? I don't think Dad should have said that but since he did, he should apologize. I mean, what's the big deal! And he might have but it was Mom's call, and she's been waiting for it for a long time. Mom and Nora from Russia never spoke to one another again. Ilene got divorced, Nora died, and Mom and Hen are still on the phone every day.

TATTOO LADIES

"I'll go home and get my panties
You go home and get your scanties
And away we'll go
Mmm-mmm-mmm
Off we're gonna shuffle
Shuffle off to Buffalo."

"Pardon me, boy, is that the Chattanooga choo choo? Whooo. Whooo!"

Mom and Ethel Fogelman are belting one out from the backseat of the car, during a Sunday drive in the countryside. I'm stuck between Gram and Dad in the front seat and Gram won't move. She won't sing either but she's good to sleep on when we drive home.

"Sing The Tattoo Lady, Mom!"

"Oh, oh," they tease, rolling their eyes like pussy cats."Have you ever heard of the tattoo lady?"

We cruise along, Mom and Ethel shimmy-shaking, and Dad quietly driving.

Gram didn't like that song, mostly the part, "She's tattoo up and down. She's tattoo round and round. But the part that I like best, is tattoo on her chest. Take me back to the rolling hills of Tennessee!"

Mom and Ethel are squealing and Dad is snorting. Not Gram - and she had a lot to shake. Her hills are higher than Mom's and Ethel's, and maybe she didn't want to start tossing those things around. I wondered if she was the lady in the song. Once, when we shared secrets, Gram told me that, before she moved to America, she worked in a circus in Russia. Meanwhile, Mom and Ethel are going on, "And on her hips, two battle ships." I could imagine those boats sailing around Gram's hips and I'm wondering how I can get a peek at them. That night, when we drove home, I curled up in Gram's hills and went to sleep, thinking about the ships going by below. I was pretty sure that she was *tattoo* - at least on her hips and chest.

Well, one day I got a peek. It happened when Gram took me to the amusement park and fell down in the rolling barrel you had to walk through at the Fun House. She's rolling around in that barrel, and everyone is yelling, "There's a lady rolling around in there. Somebody grab her!" But nobody does. They're all just standing there watching Gram roll around like an apple.

Gram didn't seem to mind much. She kept rolling around in there and, after awhile, she just got up and walked out. But while she was tumbling, her legs went over her head and I looked real hard. There were no ships in sight, so that settled that. Except, I knew then for sure that she really had worked in the circus in Russia, and her secrets were true, even if Mom said they weren't.

BIRDS OF WORRY

"That the birds of worry and care fly above your head - this you cannot change. That they build nests in your hair - this you can prevent."
- Chinese proverb

I used to wonder if I was one of those birds of worry 'cause Mom's always yelling, "Get out of my hair!" And I'm thinkin' how can I be in her hair - there's no room. Mom's hair must look good to birds of worry. First off, it looks like a cornfield. No wonder they're all flappin' around in there. They must build their nests at night when she's asleep 'cause Mom makes a lot of noise when she's awake.

Gram's hair, on the other hand, gave those birds trouble. First off, it's wound around her head in tight circles, and she puts stuff on it to harden it like a shelf. If a bird tried to get in there it would need a jack hammer - and birds don't have 'em. Must be – 'cause Gram never seems to worry about anything.

Now Dad's hair is coiled tight like little wire springs. Gram says there's no room up there for *anything*. Once I saw a bird grab one of Dad's curls and yank it like a worm. *Snap!* - the curl sprang back and blew that bird right off Dad's head. It landed on top of Gram's bird - the one with the cracked beak.

Then there's Dad's brother, Uncle Izzy. Izzy has *no* hair. His head looks like an ice pond. Gram says it's frozen very deep. I've seen birds hit it, thinking something's on the other side - and end up on their backs. I'm always glad when

28

Izzy goes home - and takes his kids with him. Enough is enough.

Anyway, now that I'm not around anymore, you'd think Mom would give up the birds. But no, and worse, I end up with hair like hers, so I'm keeping my eye out - I'm not gonna have nests in *my* hair.

NOT IN MY HAIR!

Mom used to yell, "Get out of my hair!" when she thought I was being a pest. She also liked "You're getting on my nerves" but getting in her hair was big time.

Gram's hair was wrapped around her head so tight that she didn't worry about me getting in there. With her, it was about being *a worm in her bosom*, which sounded pretty bad, so I settled on Mom's hair.

So anyway, Mom got real upset that day. She and Dad were walking into the house, and some flapping thing landed on Mom's head.

Dad said later, "Your mother really lit into that bug!"

Mom ripped it out of her hair - jumped, bashed, punched, and crunched it. Then she took it inside and flushed it.

"Where did it come from, Mom?"

"I don't know! There! Up there!" she cried, pointing to the sky outside the window.

"You could have just let it go."

"I didn't like it."

"You didn't have to kill it."

"It got in my hair."

That thing made a mistake. You don't mess with Mom's hair. I heard Mom on the phone with Ethel Fogelman.

"It was a big thing, green like a crow - or something. I don't know what it was. I never saw anything like it - and it's in my hair. So I just got it out of there."

I told my sister later, and she decided it was an alien scout from another galaxy. But that wasn't enough for her - it had come here to make peace. Feeding my sister's fury, I said it was probably making an emergency landing.

"She would do that!" Arlene howled, drawing in her lips so hard I wondered if they'd come back out again. "She beat it to death, didn't she? She'll put an end to the world, yet."

My sister was always looking for a reason to stop talking to Mom.

Mom believed she was psychic, and I'll have to admit that she seemed to know things nobody else did. When she got stuck, she went for her Ouija board. Gram worked the board, too - but I don't know how she knew what it was saying because she couldn't read English. She would rock back and forth, rolling her eyes and pushing the planchette all over the board. Then she would stop, stare at the ceiling, and start shaking like she was in a trance – and get messages about Dad. But she was nowhere near the right letters. Maybe the letters don't matter when you're in a

trance. Mom, on the other hand, knew the right letters and she had answers for everyone. I once heard someone call her a lighthouse. Her hair probably helped. Maybe that's why that thing landed on her in the first place. Whatever. My sister still isn't talking to my mother.

It turned out that Mom, like Ethel, had roots to take care of, and although my mother was not as luminous a lamp as Ethel, they both walked around with hair like spotlights. Their heads seemed to attract all kinds of things.

Well, one day I'm out walking with Mom and Dad.

Mom looks up at the sky, and says, "Look at all those birds!"

Splat! - one of them gets her. *Bull's eye!* - right on her head. After that, she stopped looking up.

ELBOW GREASE

"We don't stop playing because we grow old. We grow old because we stop playing." - Anon

When I was twelve years old, I went to work on Saturdays, to help my grandfather in his grocery store. Mostly, I smoked his cigarettes while he went to take a nap in a little room in back of the store. As soon as he closed the door, I lit up a Pall Mall.

One day, after his nap, Gramp looked around to see what I had done while he was sleeping. Then he made a face, and said we needed elbow grease. So I asked him where he kept it and he said it looked like we had run out.

"Go down the street to the hardware store, and tell Mr. Ralph that you're Mr. Morris's grandson. Tell him Mr. Morris said we need some elbow grease."

So I hopped over to the hardware store - like a big deal, to be buying something like *elbow grease*.

In a grown-up voice, I told Mr. Ralph what my grandfather said to say. Mr. Ralph made a face, and then he walked through the whole hardware store poking around in all the shelves. He took a long time, and then he told me, "Go back and tell Mr. Morris I'm all out of elbow grease."

"Well, do you have any other kind?"

"What kind do you want?"

"Maybe something that works like elbow grease."

"Nothing works like elbow grease."

"Okay. I'll tell my grandfather that."

So I went back and told Gramp what Mr. Ralph said.

My grandfather made a face, and said, "Then, Sonny, go home."

I told Gram why I came home early, and she said, "So maybe they'll get some in next week."

But they never did. There must have been a run on elbow grease because Mr. Ralph didn't get any more. Gramp never said another word about it, and I went on working for him the rest of the summer, smoking his Pall Malls while he slept.

FED UP

When Mom's *fed up* with me - "I'm just fed up!" - she starts quoting stuff from the *old testament*.

One she uses a lot is, "*When I was a child, I acted like a child but now that I'm a man, I don't do that anymore.*"

And I tell her, "I'm ten, Mom."

And she says, "It doesn't matter."

And I say, "Show me in that book where it says that."

And she says, "That's enough!"

Then she calls Hen or Ethel on the phone, "You wanna know how I feel? I'll *tell* you. I wanna choke him!"

So I tell her, "You shouldn't talk about your child like that to a stranger."

"I'm not talking to strangers, I'm talking to Hen. Go away."

"I wanna see that old testament, Mom. What's it say about choking your kids?"

BIG BOOTS

"The good-looking boy may be just good in the face." - Apache

Some people look just like their names. The principal of my elementary school is called Dr. Alice K. Liveright - and she looks like it. It's probably why she got the job - because she's smaller than I am and has tiny little shoes.

"So, why are we here *today*," she says to me.

"I don't know," I say back to the ball of hair on top of her head.

And I don't. Mom says Alice K. Liveright's gonna toss me out of that school - but she doesn't. I think she had a *good name.*

My riding counselor at camp is called Mrs. Gladys Paddock. She has a lot to say about everything *except horses* - like we have to get big boots so we can ride one. So Mom takes me to get big boots because Mrs. Paddock says they'll keep my feet warm - but they don't. They're just too big and get stuck in the stirrups. But anyway, Mrs. Paddock can run faster than the horses in *her* boots. I've seen her come out of the barn like a hockey puck, and I think it would be fun to race her. But I don't. Once I whinnied at Mrs. Paddock, and she told me not to do it again. So I just ride around in big boots all summer until camp ends. I think Mrs. Paddock had a *good name,* too. I mean she looked like what she did.

But not all names are *good ones.* I once worked with a man called *Mr. Tom Splended,* and he had blue shoes made out of snakeskin - the kind Dad called *the cat's meow.*

One day, Tom Splended says to me, "It's not *what* you are - it's what people *think* you are."

And some people in our office think he's the bull's balls because, "He *looks* good."

It's probably why he got the job.

But some others don't care much what he *looks* like, "Inside, driving that piece of scenery, is a demented little freak!"

That's a mouthful but there must have been something to it because in the end the *paint job* didn't work - and Mr. Splended didn't either. Maybe if he could have just stood around and *looked* good but that's what the plants were for. Sometimes shoes can fool you.

FAMILY MATTERS

"Truth does not happen, it just is." - Hopi

RUSHA MUSHA

Around and around we children marched in a circle behind Ilene, waving sticks and chanting, "We come from Rusha - Rusha Musha!" when an avalanche of Russian grandmothers descended from the porches of Twelfth Street to silence us.

"Shush!" they cried. "We come from nowhere! We're from here."

My sister stood at the street corner carrying her small bundle of belongings.

"Can you take me across the street?" she asked an old woman.

"And where are you *going?*" the woman asked back.

"*To Russia,*" Arlene replied. "But I'm not allowed to cross the street by myself."

And so that old Russian woman, eyeing my sister's tiny lunch pail, and knowing what a long trip lay ahead, brought my sister back to our house. Arlene didn't get to Russia that morning but she packed herself up and left the rest of us.

Mom says, "I don't know what changed between us."

Aunt Bebe says, "It was *always* like that."

My sister went away, and Mom is still waiting at the station for her to return.

PUSSY PILLOWS

"If mama ain't happy, ain't nobody happy." - *Anon.*

In the summer of 1978, I sent my parents to a craft school in the mountains of North Carolina. Dad had just retired and was breaking out in rashes and sitting in hot water all day. And nobody knew what to do with him.

"Your father's miserable," Mom said to me,

So I said to her, "Why don't you go to a craft workshop at Penland? Maybe he'll learn something new."

Dad wouldn't go, so she said, "Well, I'll go take something, and if I go then he'll go with me and I'll tell him, you'll do something so you won't be bored."

So Mom signed up for a course in fabric sculpture and Dad took jewelry making - and off they went into the mountains.

A week later I phoned to see how they were doing. Mom thought the food was so-so.

"And the workshop?" I asked.

"So-so."

So I ask my sister, "What's going on with Mom?"

And she says, "I'll let *her* tell you. She's not having a great time. But Dad loves it."

When my parents came home, I went to get them at the airport. There's Dad carrying a small box, and there's Mom dragging a long, green thing that looked like an impacted python.

"What's *that*?" I asked her.

"*That's* what I made."

"What is it?"

"It's a pea pod."

"*Why* did you make a pea pod?"

"I don't know. I just did. We had to make *something*."

"What did everyone else make?"

"They were upset about me."

"Why?"

"Well, they weren't a happy bunch. I was the oldest one and I thought I would help them. But they didn't want help. They just grumbled and kept stuffing these cushions they were making. I don't want to talk about it."

"Well, *you* didn't make a cushion."

"*No, I did not.* I did my own project. The other women were nice in the beginning but that changed. They kept to themselves, so I just worked on my pea pod - and no one seemed to like what I was doing."

"So what were they doing with the pillows?"

"What are they doing? They're stuffing these triangles and sewing fringe on them. That's what they're doing! Every one of them! I don't know *what* they're doing! They're all making - stuffing - these things and embroidering them and doing them - I don't know *what* they're doing in there! And they're carrying on about their - I don't even want to say it!"

"Vaginas?"

"Yeah. And I'm not going there. I think they had problems with those things."

"What things?"

"So I tried to talk to them. Like I said, it was okay in the beginning. But then it wasn't anymore. I don't know what's going on. But I'm not making one of those things!"

"So you sat in there, right in the middle of those women, fabricating a giant penis, and sticking them all inside it."

"I like it. I think it's cute. Look! It unzips and inside I made all these peas with smiling faces."

"They must have been rabid! You can do that, Mom."

"So? They can do what they want to. I never said a word."

"You said plenty."

"What did I say? I made a face for each woman in the group, put them in the pea pod, zipped them up - and came home. So?"

"So? There's a *name* for that, Mom."

"Creative?"

Mom never touched soft sculpture again. Dad made jewelry for the next twenty years, and had the healthiest skin in the neighborhood.

THE TOOTH OF DECEMBER

December 10, 2009

Approaching their eighties, my parents began to hold hands when they walked together. I sometimes followed behind them, watching their fingers search the air and connect. Locked together, they became smaller and more distant each year. The gate behind which I felt safe, the reins I held, were fading away.

Walking behind my parents, I shut my eyes and open them again to see if they are still before me. They always are, as I know they will be. Then, I let them get further ahead of me – and blink again. They're still there but smaller. I wonder how it feels if they are not there. Blink! There they are – every time. It's a comforting game. I know that one day they won't be there in front of me. Blink! But not today. *Blink! Blink! Blink!*

And now my father is gone. My mother's fingers find connections in the pages of books. I ask her how she's doing and she replies, "I was blue today but it passes."

"Why are you blue?" *I'll blink it away.*

"I'm an old woman," she might say, and she leaves it there.

Out walking this morning, in a hoarseness of geese I felt my parents coming. *Blink!* There - ahead of me - stamped in the landscape, they are strolling hand in hand.

FINDERS, KEEPERS

"Find out what you are and be such." - Pindar

"So you see, he loved you." My mother has discovered hidden in Dad's desk, invitations to exhibitions of my paintings.

"I see," I replied.

Mom messing with the evidence, trashing the facts. When something makes her uneasy, or blocks her intentions, she hides it in her internal trash compactor. Mom has a long relationship with toilets. "I just go a lot," she reasons, "It's not life threatening, or anything like that."

If the world does not comply, Mom declares the case closed: "Tomorrow is another day."

But on scarce occasions, she reveals traces of her past, and her reasons come home.

"My mother didn't come to my high school graduation."

"I had to wear hand-me-downs and my shoes were too tight."

"She adored my step-brother."

"I never had nice legs."

Mom's mother lived with us when I was growing up. Like her daughter, my grandmother told stories. Her marriage was lackluster - so she made things up that were better, like how she got the little holes in her ear lobes, and why she rested her teeth in a glass by her bed at night. Gram's truths lay among her pins and rings in a jewelry box that came with her from Belarus. I believed with all my heart that she wore her teeth out in Russia, carrying elephants across a high wire in a circus. Mom, however, takes her editing shears to her mother:

"She was ahead of her time. She *could have been* a fashion designer - *or something.*"

"She *was* something, Mom, she was a story-teller."

At age twenty, Mom was a looker. She played and sang in her own dance band. That was enough for Dad. When the music stopped, he had a wife, two kids and a job.

Mom concluded, "Your father had no ambition and it made problems between us. He was too young."

"Did you ever talk about it?"

"He didn't talk."

"What did you do about that?"

"*We didn't talk.*"

So how did she deal with her husband's silence? She left it in the toilet. I expect Mom married Dad to get out of her parents' house, and later, went to work to get out of our house. She preferred answers to questions.

"But he loved me. He was good to me. He bought me nice things."

"Great, Mom but – "

"One day at a time, like Scarlett O'Hara."

The case is closed.

During our Sunday drives in the countryside, Dad often wandered off, and Mom went looking for him: "I can't find your father." Dad drifted. Mom called it "lacking ambition."

We played house. Dad went to work and brought home a new car. Mom went to work and brought home dinner. Sister had a pink room. I had a dog. Dad collected stamps and coins. Mom talked on the phone. We were a pop-up picture book, like the families we knew. I was, however, a problem.

Mom recalls, "You were a mischievous kid. You were in mischief."

"How much?"

"*Enough.*"

"That's why I sent you to that school for special children - difficult."

"How was I difficult?"

"You put someone's braids is an inkwell, that's how. So again, I got a call - come to school. I did a lot of walking from our house to that school. They were days."

"How did you feel about that?"

"I'm living today. Things change over a lifetime. You don't think about the bad. You let it go. Those teachers were good. She gave you a duck. Every morning - quack! quack! I was afraid they were going to throw us out of the neighborhood."

"But they didn't."

"No. Every time that school held a meeting for parents, they would talk about a difficult child. And it was you."

"What did they say?"

"They said you had imagination. They didn't know what to do with you. I was afraid they would throw you out."

"But they didn't."

"No. They didn't."

"What happened?"

"There was this teacher. She lived on a farm, I think. She took your duck."

"And?"

"I don't remember. They kept you."

My having imagination doesn't shine Dad's shoes but medical school will. And the fight for my life starts. If that's his price, I figure it's a bad trade and the years of silence between us get going. From time to time, Mom volunteers, "He loves you. He just doesn't know how to show it. You're a lot alike."

Then she went to the toilet.

Someone decided that Dad and I should do something together - like attending football games on Saturday afternoons. I had no interest in football, so Dad bought me a little book, Terry and Bunky Play Football. I would rather lie in the path of a train than go to a football game but we went anyway. I hated the games but liked the soft pretzels. Later, lying in bed at night, I heard Dad playing Chopin nocturnes on the piano. Much as I disliked and feared the man, I had to grant him a sensitive touch, and wondered if my father was suffocating. When I mentioned Dad's piano playing to Mom, she said, "He never *finished* anything." One day, surfacing for a moment from our silence, Dad tells me he sometimes drives aimlessly for long distances - something I will learn to do as well.

I don't know why my father came to exhibitions of my paintings. He would walk through the gallery looking at the work and never saying a word to me. At my first show in New York, Dad walked around with a calculator. The gallery owner told me later that my father thanked her several times during the evening for "doing this for Ted."

"Your father's got a problem," she told me.

My sister, who, like Dad, emerged from and retreated into walls like figures in a Vuillard painting, made a rare appearance. "Dad told me, 'Ted's got it made! All he has to do when he needs money is paint a picture.' "

My failure to my father was to succeed as an artist. He fought the ambiguities that ran through him like a choppy river, and when the course of my life threatened to cause flooding in his, he sandbagged the banks. One day, from somewhere, he uncharacteristically confided, "I disappointed your mother. She wanted me to be more."

My father never learned to tell stories.

It's been said that truth lies where it is left. Dad's need to explore, his curiosity, became in me a drive to create. He might have sensed that he was leaving behind adventures that would not be his. When my father was dying, I told him *I am your son*, wanting him to know that I would carry him forward and finish the job. But Dad was already drifting. He sat in the sun listening to the geese overhead - and said nothing. And Mom? She spends her days reading books, traveling in and out of other people's stories. It's absorbing and safe. Their lives, Mom's game. If she likes a story, she can hold on to it; if she doesn't, she can dump it. Finders, keepers. Losers, weepers. Tough to do in life. It suits her.

WINDS THAT BLOW

I.

"The wind blows over the lake and stirs the surface of the water. Thus, visible effects of the invisible are manifested." - I Ching

Through the summer and fall I visit my father at Willow Lake Assisted Living Center. From a window in his room he can watch the lake and the willows that encircle it. When I arrive, Dad asks me to take him outside to the lake, where we sit feeling the sun on our faces and watching the trees bend in the wind. Sometimes we bring bread and feed the geese.

"Isn't this wonderful?" my father says, shutting his eyes.

Together we listen to summer sounds. Being alive, for him, is about feeling the sun and wind, watching birds fly and feed, listening to sounds of water and insects. "Isn't this wonderful?" *Feeling. Watching. Listening.*

"You should see them. They grew up so fast," Dad reports, when I phone, on the progress of the amaryllis plants on his window sill. They are there to get up for in the morning, and to look at before going to bed at night. *Growing. Getting up. Looking.* For my father, signs of life lay everywhere - and in the presence of my mother. He is well aware of the corrupting of his body but that is not where he chooses to dwell in his mind. "Take me outside," he says when I come to visit. I discover that my father is a poet. And I learn that I am his son, and embrace his legacy to find a peace that has eluded me all my life, as I searched for a *home place* - maybe *this* town, *this* job, *this* house, *this* person. But in the wind and the sun, the movement of trees, amaryllis bulbs, my father's windy hair and closed eyes?

II.

"Your father died this morning."

I hang up the phone and stand there not knowing what to do. My head goes into shock but my feelings do not. I turn from my head to my heart and know that the thing to do, the first step, is to go to Baskin-Robbins and have an ice-cream cone. I don't know how to approach a ritual of grieving. I need to find a form for my bereavement. I feel like a coat that has lost its hanger.

III.

"Do not stand at my grave and weep,
I am not there...
I am a thousand winds that blow....
I am not there; I did not die." - *Anon*

On a Tuesday morning in January, my father's soul and spirit leave the body that they have called home for ninety years, and find their way again to the thousand winds that blow. It is a sunless morning, and as the funeral procession is leaving the cemetery, I look back through falling snow at tree limbs pounding the windows of our car. My father wants to go home with us.

IV.

I return to Portland and walks in the woods. The wind follows. I sit and watch it animating the trees at my studio windows. It occurs to me that my father is talking to me, and I learn to read the wind. Grieving becomes receiving, as I listen to the trees. In time, they stop raging and hitting, and start sighing and touching. When the wind comes inside and reaches *my* branches, I sound back. I begin to paint. For months I paint the trees as energy and forces - as sound. My father and I are painting together, something we never did before. *Do not stand at my grave and cry, I am not there; I did not die.* I went to a funeral to bury my father and lo! he came home with me. The loss I anticipated suffering became instead a gain. The paintings that give form to this time are for me a celebration - evidence of a transfiguration of father and son from a corporeal relationship to a spiritual one - and a hanger for my coat.

FISH GOTTA SWIM

"Where do words come from?
From what rubbing of sounds are they born
on what flint do they light their wicks
what winds brought them into our mouths..."
- Venus Khoury-Ghata

Did ya see *that*!

See what?

The fish.

What fish?

Outside her door.

Outside whose door, Mom?

Hers.

Who's her?

Evelyn.

Your friend down the hall? So what's wrong with a fish?

I don't like it.

What don't you like about it?

No one else has a fish outside their door.

So?

I don't like fish.

It's a painting hanging on the wall.

Well, I think a painting of a fish on the wall is ridiculous. First of all, we didn't have paintings up at all – it was just clear.

What was clear?

Clear? The wall was clear! The only thing that people had outside their door was one thing that told who they were - and maybe a little something about them. Now she's got this painting of a fish! It's unnecessary.

Why is it unnecessary?

Because there are no other pictures on the walls.

I think it's nice.

Well, I don't think it is because everybody would put things out - and some would be nice and some would not be nice and the place would look like hell.

But the guy across the hall from you has a flag hanging on his door!

Yeah, well that isn't necessary either.

It's not necessary? What are you gonna tell people? What they can put on their doors?

At least it's on his door. Hers is on the wall in the hall!

What's the difference?

I don't know.

You just don't like her, Mother. What's that woman done to *you?*

I don't like *it!* I just don't!

You don't like *her.* It's not that fish.

Well, I don't like her because she's a phony. I did like her originally because I thought she had brains. She *is* smart. I'll grant her that.

You thought she had brains?

She does. But she's two-faced. I don't like that. The fact that she's a clever woman and she's a talented woman - I give her that! She is. You'd be surprised around here. They all went to Vassar - or someplace.

So – what do you *not* give her?

I think she's a phony! My life's been different. How many people ran off to play in a band in Chicago when they were just out of high school? I've had an interesting life.

Why is she a phony?

Because I think that she pretends that she's a good friend when she's not.

Well, what do you want from her? You told me she was looking for a guy. So she found one!

That part's okay. She can have all the boyfriends she wants. She had a boyfriend before. I don't care. This one has no legs. I don't care. I see them go in her room all the time.

Without legs?

Yeah. I don't know what she does with them in there.

What do you care *what* they do in there!!

Well, they're together all the time.

So what's that have to do with phony? She could still be your friend.

I just don't like her. You have a feeling about somebody that you just don't like. I can't express it.

You're doing a pretty good job. Look, Mom, for awhile she needed a girlfriend but she was looking for a guy.

I already had a guy - your father. He treated me well and he loved me.

She didn't want a girlfriend. She wanted a boyfriend.

It may not be about me personally. True. But I don't like her!!

So leave her fish alone.

If that fish wasn't there - you walk through the hallway - it looks quiet. Everybody has a poster on the door with their name on it. It's okay. That's enough. If I don't like it I don't like it!

What about if everyone had a fish on the wall outside their door? It would be like an aquarium.

You're a good artist, Ted, but as a lawyer, you stink.

So she stinks 'cause she dropped you for a guy!

No. *Fish* stink. She doesn't stink. She's a very smart woman.

I don't get it.

She may be smart but I think she's two-faced. I think she's dishonest. I don't like dishonest people.

Because you feel she traded you for a guy?

Oh no. That part – no - because she's still friendly to me. When we see each other it's hello – how are you. I give her the crossword puzzles out of my paper every morning. She cuts them out.

Listen, Mom, you could have a guy, too. They're all over the place.

I don't want a guy! Believe me, I've looked around. There's nothing here!

So how is she two-faced?

There's just something about her that – aren't there people who just touch you that way?

Yeah but she's not hurting you in any way. Is she?

No, she doesn't hurt me. She doesn't hurt me at all. I have my friends. I don't need her. It's just something about her that goes against the grain I think. I can't say.

So let's just go take the fish off the wall.

Why should I do that?

It bothers you that much every time you walk past it.

No. It's not my apartment! That's her apartment.

I know - but you're telling me it messes up the whole hall, and every time we walk past that painting you make some comment or stick your tongue out.

It – it – it - I don't like it!! But other people might like it. I'm not the only one that lives on this floor.

It's a nice painting.

It may be a nice painting.

If you like fish.

She's got two of them up there. The *other* painting isn't so terrible.

It's not a fish.

I don't see a *fish* hanging on the wall!

It's a nice painting.

Well, if you like it - you like it.

It adds a little color.

Okay, good. You like it; I don't!

Because you don't like her, you don't like the fish.

Well if I don't like her I can still say she's a very smart woman.

Yeah but other than that you're not saying a whole lot!

Because I think she's two-faced.

You told me that already.

That's what I don't like. I don't like people – and you don't either, I know you - you don't like people who are two-faced.

No, I don't. I like them with *one* face.

With *one* face!

Not two faces.

Right! But - that's all right. If that's good for her – it's good for her.

I'll paint a fish for you and it can be good for you, too.

If it gives her pleasure and she likes –

I think she likes pleasure.

Good. That's good. That doesn't bother me. I have my friends. If I didn't have friends and I didn't go with them and enjoy eating with them and talking to them and playing bridge with them I would say well I didn't have anybody. It's just that I don't like certain things about her. *Like the fish!*

Like the fish? Ask her to take it down. Mom, *what are we talking about?*

No I won't do that because it's her apartment. She can do whatever she likes.

But you keep telling me how offended you are every time we walk past it.

Then she'll tell me to take down *my* things, too.

She might do that.

Well, I don't want her to do that!

But she might.

I don't care what she does!

Whoa Mom!

It's a good thing you didn't go into law, Ted.

I don't understand.

You take dislikes to some things - and if you don't like them, you don't like them. I know you!

True, Mom

True, Ted

So I guess you got it from me.

Yeah. Well. I think it's a nice painting of a fish, that's all.

So it's a nice painting of a fish. Let her keep it in her apartment. I don't care. Or - I can put *this* out there or I can put *this* out there. *I* can put a painting out there.

So why don't you?

'cause I don't want to!!!

Come on, Mom, if the guy across the hall puts a flag on the wall -

On his door.

On his door.

And that's silly, too.

What's silly about it?

Because it doesn't need this big flag draped there.

But *he* does. It's his door.

But it's not on the wall.

Wall! Door! What's going on here?

Okay, so you win the argument.

I'm not trying to win the argument. But look, people love different things. You must love that red sweater you've got on all the time, even if it's got a big hole at the elbow.

It's a good sweater. I got it at Brooks Brothers.

Well, if it means so much to you, why don't you hang it out on the wall?

With the hole showing! You see, that makes me *different*. I go along with a holy sweater.

Well your girlfriends don't like it. They put a donation box in the dining room.

Yeah, I know. They sent letters around asking for contributions. I look at her and she looks like *a drowned rat*.

Who?

Evelyn. She's always with the man who has a blanket over his lap. And before him there was another man. And before him there was another man. She was married three times.

And that makes her a drowned rat?

I thought she was a different kind of person. She's - there's just something about her I don't like!

You have to have a reason.

I don't have a reason.

Maybe you don't like the color of her hair - or something.

Maybe she doesn't like the color of *my* hair. So what should I say?

Her hair's the same color as yours! That wouldn't stand up in a court of law.

I think she's an opportunist. That's what I don't like.

Well she is.

She is - but I don't like that in people.

She looks out for herself, Mom.

A lot of people do.

So she hung out with you 'til she found a boyfriend - and that's what she was looking for.

That's okay.

And she'd rather be with him. That's what I think this is all about.

Now - I have to go to the bathroom. She's crafty.

Crafty? I think you don't like her 'cause you feel like she dropped you when she met that guy.

Oh no, that doesn't bother me because I have good friends here. I don't need *her*.

I don't get what you're talking when you tell me she's crafty. What it has to do -

I can't explain it.

I know you can't. I keep asking. When you figure it out, call me.

I'm not the only one that feels that way. That's why I can't explain it.

Maybe someone else can. Who can we ask?

Nobody, Ted.

Well, she is what she is.

That's right. She is what she is.

Now look, Mom, if Joe across the hall can have a flag on his door - If her fish was on the door instead of the wall would that make it okay?

Yeah, I guess.

Mother – *no it would not!*

Okay, let her have her fish. She's got another big picture there, too.

So?

Well, if she wants to have an art gallery out there -

So - is that so terrible?

Then put some *good* art up!

What's wrong with a fish? She painted a nice fish. C'mon -

Okay, Ted.

Okay, what? You don't like the way the way she painted it?

I don't like a fish hanging on the wall.

It's a nice fish.

You like it?

I think it's a trout.

I don't know *what* it is!

It looks like a trout.

No, it's not a trout. Maybe it's a barracuda. Yeah.

You think it's a barracuda?

Maybe but you gotta see the teeth. I can't see the teeth. Its lips are closed – just like hers.

Well its teeth must be in there somewhere.

Yeah. *She's smart.*

I don't know what that has to do with anything. She's smart but she's crafty and she's a fake – and a barracuda. Come on, Mother, what's the problem?

You think she's such a *little thing.* She's had three husbands. Now she's got this man. Before this man she had another man here. Something about her. She reminds me– remember the woman who was the Prince of Wales' mistress – and he married her – the Duchess of Windsor!

But there are people like that.

I guess there are! But I don't care. I can say what I want. If I like her or don't like her I can say it.

Where were *you* when the Prince was looking? How come *you* didn't snatch him? You're prettier than she was. And you're prettier than the rat down the hall.

Ha! I thought he was horrible. That's not my taste. And she's not either.

But she had *three* husbands?

Who? The Duchess of Windsor?

No. The fish lady.

Yeah, she did.

I ran into her early this morning getting coffee in the cafeteria.

She gets it for *him*. She takes him his coffee."

That's nice.

And she has a daughter that's an artist who had a show here of pictures she takes.

That's nice.

Yeah. But the pictures were - every - each one - looked the same.

Were they of fish?

No.

Hey, Mom, What's going on here? *Where are we?*

That's *enough*. Let's go get some lemonade.

Lemonade? Mom? We're not finished!

I'm finished.

WORKING DAYS

"What the people believe is true." - Anishinabe

SET FREE

Winston-Salem, North Carolina, 1964

"Sometimes, not too far off, she would stage another rebellion. It would not be the same kind of rebellion, though. One could never repeat the real adventures....whereas, it only they had the courage to push on, forward...they would sometimes make new discoveries as bright as the others, or even brighter, perhaps."

I needed a job. It seemed that at the end of the school year, *budget considerations* called for the elimination of *one* teacher, and once again it was me. I liked teaching but was beginning to think that something didn't like me, and was pretty sure it wasn't the students. Anyway, I heard that an experimental school in Winston-Salem, North Carolina was looking for teachers, went for an interview, and got hired for the summer. So in June of 1964, I bought "a good lookin' car for 300 bucks," moved out of New York City, and with a worn-out dream beside me, drove south. In the rearview mirror, I watched the last four years dissolve away into what hadn't happened. Done.

Welcome to New Jersey, and Washington, and Virginia. Teacher - you're in North Carolina - Greensboro - Winston-Salem - East Fifth Street - and the parking lot of an abandoned city hospital - home of the North Carolina Advancement School, where I was going to teach English. My stomach hurt, and I was already lonely. And then there occurred one of those incandescent moments that seem to come from nowhere and change everything. I heard a boy's thin voice call out, "Reckon that's him!" and knew that North Carolina would be more than a summer in my life. I turned to the dream riding with me - but it had already died.

Room and board came with the job and, after settling into my room down the hall from the hospital Admissions Center, I walked over to the porch of the director's house to meet the chairman of the English Department.

"Mr. Katz?"

"Yes."

"How do you do? I'm Dr. Nickels, and this is Mrs. Huggums, who will be one of your colleagues."

"Hello," I offer.

Silence.

"You're different from what we were expecting."

That didn't take long. A budget crisis. *One* job's gotta go.

"How so?" I try.

"Well, more – different," Dr. Nickels smiles.

Mrs. Huggums looks at Dr. Nickel's, and then she smiles, too. So I smile as well and there we three stand - smiling. Nickels loses her balance for only a moment and we proceed to *make conversation*. Huggums is another story.

Her eyes are batting back and forth like a shuttlecock from me to my red, white and black Buick with extended glass-packed dual mufflers. That night I don't sleep. I'm scared because I need this job, don't want to mess up, and Mrs. Huggums' eyes are crawling all over the room, trying to get out.

The following morning, the English Department met with a *consultant* to design an *experimental* curriculum. Dr. Noose arrives, nods a lot, rocks back and forth, makes diagrams, produces an experimental curriculum and zips out of there to catch her flight back to New Hampshire. We're going to teach English by way of either mythology, oceanography, or farm animals. Pick one. Dr. Noose has no doubt that mythology or oceanography will motivate the boys like magnets. And farm animals? A natural - guaranteed to appeal to the farmer in every Southern boy. I don't think so but, as I've said, I need the job. And I'm supposed to be a *master teacher* who will work with two regional teachers-in-residence, Lib Huggums and Viola Route, who have come to live at the school for three months. That night at supper in the school cafeteria, Viola arrives wrapped like a Vegas show girl, explaining that the drapes in her room are too pretty to hang over a window. She took them down, "did a little work on them," and wore them to dinner - "I love the material." Viola Route scored huge with me that night. We're off to a roaring start!

"How about oceanography to start with?" Mrs. Huggums has never heard of it but why not. Dr. Nickels suggests we decorate our classrooms to make them inviting. Mrs. Huggums runs home to get her collection of star fish and sand dollars, and we hang them from strings attached to the ceiling. Mrs. Route, rising to the challenge, spreads sand all over the floor. She gets a little over excited with the sand but being as how that's her nature we let her run with it. Mrs. Huggums thinks it "certainly looks invitin'." - and we wait for the boys to arrive. Twenty-five of them come through the door like a shot gun blast, and start hitting the floor.

"Shit!"

"Whoa!"

Stunned disbelief. Scrambling for seats. Silence.

"Hi, I'm Mr. Katz, and - *hey!* who took those sand dollars?"

"Those *what?*" from the chorus.

"Those things that were hanging from the ceiling."

Silence.

Mrs. Route has spread her ample self across the door, apparently to prevent the criminals from escaping. Mrs. Huggums is kneading her fists into her thighs.

"Hey, Mr. Cat, don' theh all clean these rooms? Wuz awhl this stuff own the floah? I neah busted mah ass."

"Yeah, mah ass, too."

A chorus of "busted asses" tells me *a budget cut* is coming. I'm in trouble.

"All right, guys, kill it!"

Chorus, *"Kee-il whut,* Mr. Cat?"

Soloist, "Mah daddy's got him a shotguhn."

I need to do something. "This isn't going to be like any other English class you've had."

Soloist, "Whuz it gonna be?"

"We're going to study about farm animals."

Chorus, *"About what!"*

"And oceanography."

Soloist, "Wuz thet las' un?"

Mrs. Huggums, "Oshunorphagee."

"Oceanography," I add.

Mrs. Huggums looks confused.

"Anyway, we're going to learn about it."

Soloist, "Y'all tawk funny. Ain't you furrin?"

"Ain't I what?," I croak.

Chorus, "Furrin'."

"I don't understand what you're saying."

Soloist, "Well, we don' unnerstan' y'll either. Wheah ya'll from?"

"New York."

Chorus, "A Yankee!"

I look to Mrs. Route, busy blocking the door like a goal post, then to Mrs. Huggums, figuring she speaks their language - no good, she's looking like a fish on ice - and finally at my watch.

"Looks like the period has flown by. You're dismissed."

"Bah, cat!"

"Quit shovin'."

"Who took them san' thangs?"

Chairs scraping. Sand scratching. Boys hitting the floor.

"Sonuvabitch!"

"I bust mah ass on thet stuff!"

They're gone. Mrs. Huggums is pulling limp strings from the ceiling, and I'm thinking, what if she got unglued? I suggest we take a break and meet later to talk about what happened. Then I head to do a load of laundry before returning to New York. I decide to stay another day. I need this job.

The rest of the week isn't much better, and I decided even Neptune isn't going to get these kids to jump. So I go see Dr. Nickels and tell her the consultant's plan isn't working for me. Dr. Nickels goes on about stuff like encoding and decoding, cognitive and affective, and mostly her twenty years in India - and gives me a plant for my room. At the time, I think she's meaning *effective,* when she's talking about *affective,* and carry the plant back to my room wondering how Dr. Nickels thinks this stuff we're doing is effective. By the end of the second week, the boys and I are bored and frustrated. There's no vital energy between us. So I go back to talk to Dr. Nickels.

"I can't teach this way. The kids are unhappy, and I'm unhappy."

To my surprise, she says, "What do you suggest?"

"I'm not sure but I would like to be left alone with my classes to figure it out. No observers. No lesson plans. I want them to look forward to class. Let me experiment. I'll keep a log of what I do. "

So Hazel Nickels gave me an isolated classroom in what used to be the maternity ward. It looked out over the city and I liked being in it immediately. Dr. Nickels gave me the outlines she gave to all the teachers but stayed out my classroom and looked the other way. Perhaps I touched something in her. Maybe the spirit that once whisked her off to India. Whatever. I am grateful for her silence. Hazel Nickels evidently needed a job, too. But she set me free.

I enter my classroom, and two boys are fighting so I climb up on top of a desk, and sit there watching the fight. Then, while they continue to fight, I put a jazz record on the phonograph I've set up earlier in the day, and sit there reading a <u>Classics Illustrated</u> comic book. The boys keep fighting but the sounds in the room are changing. I remain absorbed in the comic book but my ears are watching - and waiting.

"Hey, man, cool it!"

"Wuz he readin' up theah?"

"Whah ain't he stoppin' the fight?"

Some finger popping to the music. Less scuffling. I keep reading the comic. Silence. I look up at an army of puzzled eyes.

"Finish your fight. I want to finish my comic."

"Whah're y'all readin'? A comic?"

"Because that's what I want to do."

"Whut're y'all readin'?"

The circle of eyes moves in. I feel a flush of excitement. A boy sticks his head under the cover of the book.

"He readin' The Invisible Man."

"Oh ah know they stoery!"

"Yeah, ah saw thet movie."

I say, "This is a different story. You probably don't know it."

"Oh yeah?"

"Yeah," I answer.

"Ah *know* thet stoery."

"You don't look like you know it."

"WHAT!"

From somewhere, *"What's* it about, Charlie?"

The eyes face Charlie.

"It's about this gah who..."

and he proceeds with his telling until,

"No, it wuz 'iz waf..."

and,

"He din't have no waf..."

and,

"Hey, y'all forgot thet 'ol lady who..."

"Uh uh, he..."

And the air explodes with hands.

"HEY, MR. CAT!"

Their energy is refocused - and I go for it.

"I should have brought that *great record* I have of this story but I guess since we're an English class I should pass out some books now."

"OH NO!"

"Ah cain't read."

"Wheah thet record at?"

"We want to heah thet record."

"It might be in my office, but I can't walk out of here. You'll tear the room apart."

"*NO WE WON'T!*"

"Get thet record, Mr Cat."

I look at the boys. The boys look back at me.

"How many want to hear that record?" I ask.

Again, the room explodes with hands.

"OK."

I get the record and two kerosene lamps.

"Let's push the desks out of the way and spread out on the floor - fast - we don't have much time left."

"We'll skip ouah next class."

"You'll skip nothing but out that door when the bell rings. Now let's do this right. *You* - pull down the shades, please. Charlie, get the lights, will ya?"

There we sat in a quiet circle, in darkness.

"*You*, will you please light the kerosene lamps?"

"Now, close your eyes and use your imagination. Imagine you're all alone in a big old empty house out in the country, and it's late at night and storming outside. If anyone is too scared, he can leave now."

"O.K."

My classroom is transformed into a turbulent thunderstorm. I watch the boys, their eyes shining in the dark. The defiance is gone from their faces. I like them. The period is about to end so I stop the record at a suspenseful point in the story.

"Oh no! Don't stop!"

"Time to go! I'll see you tomorrow morning at eight sharp!"

"We'll stay."

"You'll go."

I leave the lights out and the lamps burning - and my disgruntled class stumbles out into the hallway, their complaints muted by the sounds of thunder. No "busted asses" today. The following morning, everyone was on the floor waiting at 7:45 when I arrived for class. The lights were out - and so were matches waiting to light the lamps.

The next day, I ask them to draw pictures of the five characters in the story. They balk a bit but agree to spend the period drawing by lamplight while listening to a recording of storms. We share the drawings and laugh together. The next day, I bring to class copies of the Classics Illustrated comic books of The Invisible Man, which I've been able to round up around town. We compare an illustrator's vision to our own perceptions, sharing opinions and allowing differences. The boys agree, over the weekend, to write a horror story no more than one page long.

"Ah cain't write."

"Do you *want* to make up a story?"

"Yes."

"Then just write down the words like they sound. That's okay."

Everyone brought a story to class, and read it aloud. It was a good week.

And I began to learn that new encounters must be fresh to be vital, to respect the difference between genuine and fake - and when to start all over again. The head of a large foundation for grants told me once that such an approach was *labor intensive*. I replied that *life* is labor intensive, and the requested funding did not follow. We each had our reasons.

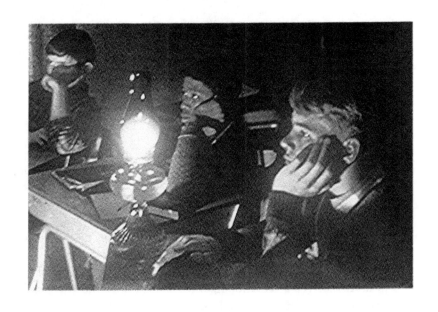

CAT AND MOUSE

Philadelphia, September, 1967

Loren Gonzales came late the first day of class, climbed on the back of a chair, watched for awhile, and walked out. By the end of the week, Loren stopped coming to my class. He was twelve years old and small for his age. In time I will call him Mouse, and he will call me Cat. *But not yet.*

The Pennsylvania Advancement School was an experimental school exploring ways to encourage junior high school boys who were performing poorly in traditional schools. It was often a pretty tough call for the teachers but I needed a job. Over the years, there would be *many jobs*, many students, and many stories. This is a small story about a small boy.

Loren wandered in and out of classes. Nothing seemed to hold his interest. I watched for keys to engaging his attention. His eyes were intensely alert. He appeared energetic and restless - more impish than detached. One of the boys told me Loren liked to draw pictures of big cats, and one of the school secretaries told me Loren liked to *pick* at her typewriter. I started carrying a sketchbook around the building, sometimes making quick drawings of students. Boys told me that Loren also drew and that he was good. Loren stayed away but I suspected he might be somewhere, watching.

Days went by. Loren began to approach the students watching me draw but quickly retreated if I so much as glanced in his direction. The boys kept telling me how good Loren could draw, and I showed little interest, appearing completely absorbed in my own efforts. I stopped looking for Loren - *but I could feel his eyes.* Then, one morning, one of Loren's friends asked me to draw his picture. I did, and gave the drawing to him. Several days later the boy brought me a drawing of three panthers. He said that Loren had made it. I told him I thought it was good and gave it back to him. He returned soon with another of Loren's drawings and told me I could keep it if I liked it. I kept it.

The following week, Loren and some of his friends made a book filled with stories about animals. Loren did the illustrations and cover. I found a copy on my desk with a note from Loren asking if I liked the drawings. He mentioned that the boys liked his work but it probably wasn't very good. I typed Loren a formal letter, telling him that I liked the drawings, and added *playfully*, that there was a rumor going around that he was not drawing much these days and had just about given up. I concluded that he was surely the best judge of his interests but it seemed a pity to me that he would draw no more. I sealed the letter in an envelope, addressed it to Loren in care of the school., and had it delivered to him by a school secretary. Later that day, the same secretary delivered to me a letter from Loren:

DEAR TED

I WANT TO TELL YOU WHY PEOPLE TELL YOU

I DONT DRAW

THE ONLY REASON I SOMETIMES DO IT IS

BECAUSE

SO OFTEN PEOPLE COME UP TO MEAND SAY

"PLEASE DRAW ME

A PICTURE SO

THATS IT

MOUSE

SORRY FOR THE BAD

TYPEING

I replied, via secretary, that his reason for not drawing wouldn't work for me but I accepted his decision. I was sure it was a good one for him. I wished him good luck in whatever he decided to do. Two more letters came from Loren - now Mouse - that week, by secretary. They were confused *peckings* that seemed to indicate that he was trying to figure out what move to make next. I decided he was testing both of us, in an effort to determine whether this game was total nonsense or something more - trying to flush out some rules, or clues. It was my move. I had tapped into his interest in drawing and typewriters. How to challenge the alertness and curiosity so evident in his eyes. I, too, was confused as to where to go with this game. I wanted to avoid sliding into a silly exchange of words that became tiresome. I didn't know what to do next - how to answer Loren's two letters - and decided to do nothing. Wait, and wonder how Mouse would react.

Well, react Mouse did! The next morning, the director of the school, looking both amused and bewildered, approached me with a letter. Mouse had given it to him, demanding irately that he deliver it to me:

dEAR MR KATES

IF YOU HAVE ALREADY SAW HE OTHER LETTERS

I EXPECTED AN ANSWER.

THESE THERES ARE TRUE SO IF ANOTHER ONE
OF THEM PEOPLE BUG ME

AGAIN IM REALLY GONNA STOP DRAWING

SOME OF THE PEOPLE AIN'T THAT BAD

DONT GET WE WRONG NOW TED I ENJOY
DRAWING

BUT IV'E BEEN DRAWING FOR ABOUT SIX OR
SEVEN YEARS

SO THIS IS HOW I FELLT ABOUT IT

WHAT DO YOU EXPECT ME TO DRAW EVERY
SECOND

FRIEND

GONZALES

Mouse was asking for a friendship. He was determining a
new game, throwing the challenge right back in my lap! I'd
been watching Mouse and picking up some insights into his
behavior. So I answered his letter telling him that I didn't
know what I expected him to do every second but I had
seen him around and had some hunches about him. I didn't
miss his tricks. I was on to him. I signed the letter, THE
PHANTOM WHO SEES ALL. I figured he knew little

about me and it might be time to begin to even the score. During the next few days, I moved about the building amplifying my interactions with others, joking and being who I was - but louder and more conspicuously. It was Mouse's turn to takes notes. And he did. When I arrived at school one morning, there was a letter on my desk:

SMART ALECK TED

I WANT TO TELL YOU

WAT OPP'S SPELLED THAT WHAT WRONG

IWANT TO TELL YOU WHAT I THINK OF YOU

1TRIEING TO BE DON'WON WITH GIRLS

2TRICK'Y

3VERY INTELAGENT

4trieing to say you 17 TEEN

THATS ALL

TRIE TO GUESS WHO WROTE THIS

IF YOU DO YOU WIN A   100000000 point's

Mouse had discovered that I liked to play, and was himself playing. I replied to his letter that *I had been found out!* We both knew that I really wasn't that young anymore and probably looked like a fool trying to flirt but some unknown person had sent me a letter and pointed all this out to me. The end must be in sight! I addressed the letter to: UNKNOWN (CARE OF MOUSE G.) Through this tongue-in-cheek reply, I was hoping to engage Mouse's wry sense of humor by adding a playful spin to our correspondence. I had worked before with troubled kids Mouse's age and found that sometimes by playing in and out of their threatening realities, it was possible to chip away with them at what was blocking their growth. It was a hunch. I was flying wild but it felt right to me. I wondered how Mouse might react to a letter in which I expressed concern over my self-image. His reply came within the hour:

DEAR DON

BOY ARE YOU OUTTA YOUR ROCKER

THOUGH HATH UNDER ESTAMATED THYSELF

THE WORD IS WAR

UN KNOWN

I learned from people at the school who had observed Mouse that he was hyperactive and clever but acutely shy, and often withdrawn. I thought about the ways in which I coped with some of the frustrations and disappointments in my life that threatened to eclipse my personal growth, and decided to encourage Mouse's interest in drawing. I made my office unconditionally open to him, and often entered to find him looking through the picture books of animals I left lying about. From time to time, a book disappeared. I said nothing, and later it reappeared. The only verbal exchange between us continued to be "hello" and "goodbye."

And then the school was preparing for a special event - Casino Day. I was painting a mural of dancing girls to hang behind the gaming tables. The teacher, who was posing for me, had to leave before I finished drawing her legs, and because it's my habit to draw directly from a live model, I was struggling to get the legs to look right. I sat down in front of the mural and stared unhappily at the unconvincing legs. And then Mouse was there. "I need you, Mouse. I can't get the legs to come out right." He picked up a piece of charcoal and quickly drew the legs. Throughout the rest of the week, we worked together on the murals. Mouse began to come to my class every day and helped out with whatever I could find for him to do. The letters, however, continued. The day before Christmas vacation, I found a letter on the driver's seat of my car:

dear Mr. ted kates

I want to tell you

something that needs

not that many words

this letter will always

prove how much friend

can be and I know I

will never forget

you and many

others too

so have a

Merry

Christmas

and a

Happy New Year

Too

Mouse was drawing all the time. His science class was working with mice and, together, we drew them in costumes from different periods of history. I stopped dropping by the class but Mouse, intrigued by the mice, continued to attend the class every day. He became interested in anatomy and went on to make detailed drawings of animal skeletons. The next thing I'm told, Mouse is working independently on drawings of human skeletons and musculature. One day, I asked him if he could help me with something. "I would like to but I have to get to class." On another day, I complimented him on a drawing of one of his classmates. "It's a beginning, Cat," he replied.

Each class of boys attended our school for only one semester, and then returned to their regular schools. At the graduation ceremony, I saw Mouse and held up a new sketchbook I had brought for him. He looked back from among the graduates, and smiled. Another class was moving on and, as always, I left school that day feeling a kind of emptiness. On the driver's seat of my car I found an envelope, on which was typed:

to

a

close

friend

And inside, a letter:

d e a r theodore kat es

i want to say goodbye but

please dont   forget me

i shared my friendship

with you and iwant tobid you

farewell

with closes friendship

Mouse gonzales

I started the motor, and looked up but couldn't see out. Printed with chalk in large letters across the front windshield I read:

THAT DAY I SAID I WAS NOT GOING TO DRAW ANYMORE WAS A MISTAKE

DREAMCATCHER

Santa Fe, New Mexico, 1972

The Lakota (Sioux) believe both good dreams and nightmares float in the air and a dreamcatcher - a willow frame strung with sinew - can screen out nightmares and let only good dreams pass through a center hole. Bad dreams are trapped in the web, where they perish in the light of dawn.

Pow! Pow! Pow! I've been assassinated! Shot from behind! I crumble at my desk, and sprawl there waiting for whatever happens after one has been killed. The penetration of the bullets was painless. I expect death to be different but feel unchanged. Me, only lighter. It's not bad, and considering that I won't have to work here after all, I feel relieved. But after being killed, what do I do next? I grope my back feeling for the bullet holes, and can't find them. There's no blood on my hands - probably a clean perforation. Staggering out of my office into the men's bathroom, I turn in front of a mirror, searching for holes in my back - just to see how big they are. No holes. I take off my sweater and hunt through it. How can there be no holes? Stunned, I wobble back to my desk.

Knock! Knock! Knock! A woman is standing in the doorway to my office.

"It's late and your lights were on. Are you all right?"

I'm in the Administration Building of the Institute of American Indian Art, where I've been engaged to improve deteriorating relations between students and teachers, and I don't know how. I'm blocked, far from home, and need the job.

"I think I fell asleep."

"I'm Imogene Goodshot.," she says, and vanishes.

Startled, I lock up and head for the parking lot. My car is the same color as the night and I can't find it. I think I see Imogene Goodshot ahead of me. "Hello," I call, walking towards her, "I've lost my car." But it's a cottonwood tree. How did she do that? And I wake up - late for work.

To my surprise, when I arrive at my office, I find a clay cup on the desk, with the word *begin* carved into its belly. I decide to get out on campus and look for Imogene Goodshot.

"Do you know Imogene Goodshot?," I ask a student.

She smiles. "Who is Imogene Goodshot?"

There's a powwow that night, and I go, hoping to find Imogene Goodshot in the women's dances. Slowly, with measured steps, the women are circling round. No Imogene Goodshot. One by one, two by three, women are drawn like threads from the onlookers, and spun into the circle as it turns and swells. No Imogene Goodshot. Round and round, more women are sucked into the fever of the thickening circle - a rope of night. Tap, tap, tap. Tap, tap, tap. Round and round. Tap, tap, tap. Tap, tap, tap.

Pow! From that cord of drums and dust and fire, Imogene Goodshot appears, a resplendent spark, and is gone.

Pow! My past lets go and falls away like a used skin.

Pow! I *arrive* at the Institute of American Indian Art.

DOUBLE BUBBLE

"I am king of the wild horses.
My life is full of splendor."
- Student graffito

Around the corner from the house I grew up in there was the Fleer's Double Bubble Gum factory, and the pink scent of bubble gum charged the neighborhood. Every store had a fishbowl full of gum by the cash register. They cost a penny a piece, and each was wrapped in bright paper twisted at the ends - a fragrant cube that you bit into and got a sweet squirt and sniff at the same time. We all wanted one going on in our mouths; it was a sign of belonging. The smell of that bubble gum stayed with me a long time. Years later, I directed a project for The Ford Foundation at the Institute of American Indian Arts in Santa Fe, New Mexico. The first grant money I spent was for cartons of bubble gum. And this is how it happened.

I had been asked by the IAIA's director, Lloyd Kiva New, to look into ways to improve declining relationships between students and teachers, and it didn't take me long to conclude that I hadn't a clue. I needed to find a way into the life of the school. Lost and lonely, I drove into town each night to Furr's Cafeteria, and sat there among paintings of orange mesas, waiting for insights. The chicken fried steaks and egg custards were comforting but something in the very air in that place was working on me. It turned out to be more than the garlic bread. Before leaving, I always lingered at the cash register, chatting with the cashier and breathing in the perfume rising from a bowl of penny bubble gum that sat on the counter.

"Cold out there tonight," she would say. "Bundle up."

"That bubble gum smells good," I would say.

"Take a piece," she would say, and I would drop one into my pocket as I left the cafeteria. Like the chicken fried steak, it comforted me.

Meanwhile, I was getting more conversation from the cashier at Furr's than from the students and staff at IAIA. They didn't talk - at least not to me. I was starting to wonder if they *did* talk. Then, one day, I'm walking around campus chewing a wad of that gum, and someone comes over and says, "Where'd you get the bubble gum?"

"I pick 'em up in town at the cafeteria."

"Got any more?"

I didn't. *But the kid could talk,* so I figured he might have more to say. I knew I couldn't begin to do anything at that school until I knew what people cared about - and I believed the students could tell me.

That night, after dinner at the cafeteria, I found out from the cashier where the gum came from, ordered several cartons, bought a fishbowl - and charged The Ford Foundation. When the gum arrived, I filled the bowl, put it on my desk in the Administration Building, stuffed all the gum I could get into my mouth, and walked around campus chewing 'til my jaw hurt. It didn't take long.

"Where'd you get the gum?"

"There's a bowl of them in my office."

"Where's that?"

"Over there. Just walk in and take a piece."

Then I went back to my office and sat at my desk *busily doing nothing* while students came and went throughout the day taking pieces of bubble gum. At first it was grab and go! But sometimes they stood and talked for awhile. I stayed out of their way - watching and listening - adjusting to them visually and emotionally. It wasn't long before a student sat down in one of the office chairs, and I saw another look around for a chair to sit in. And guess what?

The next day, I went shopping in town and found a *bean bag chair* - a big, colorful sack filled with Styrofoam beads.

"Try it out," the saleswoman said. "Everybody loves 'em."

So I cuddled into it, and sat for awhile watching the other shoppers.

"I could sit in this all day," I told her.

"So why don't you buy it?" she said.

I did, and the following morning brought it to my office. The first student who wandered in parked in it and stayed. The next gum seeker popped a piece into her mouth, and stood staring at the student in the bean bag chair. *More chairs, I thought* - ordered a dozen - and charged The Ford Foundation. Soon that room was *alive* with students coming and going - *and talking*. First to arrive each day got into the bean bags, and they were in no hurry to get back out again. I sat at my desk scribbling and listening, and hoped the students would sense that if I was not like them, I was at least not against them. And that's how it began.

I suspected many of the staff questioned what I was *doing* in there but Lloyd Kiva New knew. And I figured if I worried about what they might think at The Ford Foundation when charges showed up for bubble gum and bean bags, I might have been less open to allowing a direction to find me. What was happening *felt* right to me, as it does when I'm painting and the most vital paintings *lead me*. The students at IAIA lead me. They talked; I listened - and my work there began.

THE BREATH OF A CANDLE

"This is for you," she said, handing me a tiny bottle. "It's the breath of a candle and holds a wish. When you're ready, break the tape across the top and release your wish. But you get only one." Because I knew she was feeling ambushed at the Institute of American Indian Art, as she had on the Reservation and, later, at Reed College, I offered her my wish. "It's for you," she said, so I told her I'd wait.

Heading out of Santa Fe on her bicycle, Marilyn Antelope was struck down by a truck on Cerrillos Road. Months later when I left the Institute I took the wish with me.

I spent the winter of 1975 in the mountains of Arkansas, walking a dog and waiting. One day a man in the music store told me I ought to learn to pick a banjo, so I picked one out.

"Now you're gonna want some lessons from Johnny Taylor."

"Where's he at?"

"Just ask around. You'll find him. "

I found him in a hollow outside town, and passed some good days with The Reverend John Taylor, drinking chicory coffee while he sang gospel. But I didn't learn much how to play the banjo, except for one song - Cripple Creek.

And one day, I'm sitting on a curb at the gas station waiting for my car to get fixed, picking that song, when a big white Cadillac pulls over and a lady leans out the window and drops a dollar bill on me.

"Very nice," she says.

"Lady, I don't need this! Take it back!"

"Don't be shy," she waved, and drove away.

Now I *could* use the car, I thought, but she hadn't offered that. I could come back with a hat and maybe make a little money. But I didn't because that's not what I was in Arkansas for. I was still carrying Marilyn's little wish bottle in my coat pocket, and one day just broke the seal and let the wish out of there. I'm no trapper, so I figured that wish ought to be free to make its own wish. A few months later, I took a job in Portland, Oregon as Deputy Director of the Oregon Art Institute, and found myself *again* embedded in a theater of personal power and ambition. Daily walks helped me keep things in perspective.

One rainy afternoon, I found a carousel.

"All aboard!" the carousel man called, waving me on.

I didn't see anybody I knew, so I hopped on a bright horse and wound my arms about its neck. Around and around we turned together - a blur of longing and freedom. Don't stop, horse! Fly! As I walked away, the carousel man quietly called to me, "They get on all the time looking like you *did*, and get off looking like you *do*. Come back. By the way, the horse you rode is called Freely."

I went to work every day, and rode the carousel during my lunch break. That turned out to be a good thing because work went around in circles that seemed to go nowhere and I could have concluded that's the way things are if not for Freely, who went around in circles that seemed to go everywhere. I held on to his loops of mane, rubbed the jewels in his bridle - and went back to work. That's how I got through the job - "Get on looking like you *did* and get off looking like you *do*."

Friends asked, "How do you deal with all *that stuff* at work?"

I never told them.

Then I had a strange dream. I dreamed a child poking around a little town. Like the carousel horses, she seemed to be everywhere and not at the same time. Everyone in town knew her. They called her Vertigo Scrubber. I couldn't get that dream out of my head, so the next day I went and told the carousel man.

"Verti Scrubber, of course!" he laughed, "*You're* a scrubber with vertigo - going around in circles scouring your life! The child has come to help you. Let her *be*."

It occurred to me that I might have made a wish when I let the candle's breath go. Marilyn Antelope, Carousel Man, and Vertigo Scrubber were all special *beings* who had come into my life. There could be something going on. Each night I dream back Vertigo Scrubber, hoping to find out what she wants but she's playing hide and seek with me and I can't catch her. Like the tail of a garden snake, she's gone before she's here, leaving only a green light. Go. *Where?*

"Wait up!" I shout to Verti Scrubber. It's hard to see where she ends and the road starts. "Wait up. I'm tired of running."

But it's Marilyn Antelope, not Vertigo Scrubber, who turns to face me.

"That was a big wish you made. It took three of us."

Then she's gone - a loop of ink on the night.

"All aboard!" the Carousel Man cries and I woke up.

"Ah, what a dusty answer gets the soul when hot for certainties in this our life."
– Wm. Shakespeare

DARK HORSE

Philadelphia, Christmas, 1976

Faced with unassailable credentials for the art teaching position they were seeking to fill, the Sisters of Holy Truth College, suggested hopefully that God wanted me to go on painting rather than teach art at Holy Truth.

"That's an imposing vote of confidence," I acknowledged, "but I want to teach."

We sat in howling silence. The interview was over. The Lord's interests sealed the meeting and I continued to look for a job.

Like The Little Match Girl, I struck all the matches for a big fire. And when the light went out, I was alone, with no savings and no job. A romance in the mountains of western North Carolina ended badly. The affair was an unsustainable flight, and when the air thinned it lost altitude. My compass was set for *flying* - not building. The relationship ran aground with as much force as it went up. One wet night, we both drove away, dragging U-Hauls in opposite directions. On my long drive from Asheville to Boston, I left behind forever the person I was not.

"You're exactly what they're looking for," she exclaims, a cheerful yellow dress, coming from behind her desk like a sunrise.

"Where is this place?" I ask.

"In Philadelphia," she replies. "The Philadelphia Museum of Art. They're looking for someone with broad experience in creating public programs. A fresh face. New directions."

"I have no training in art history."

"You're what they need. It's perfect. They would be lucky to get you. I'll set up an interview. It's a great job. And a good placement for us."

Waving her folder, she darts about the office like a Good Fairy. It's an image that remains in my mind for months. But when I return some time later to visit, she doesn't look like that anymore. I wonder what the life span of a fairy is.

I grew up in Philadelphia, in awe of the Art Museum - a formidable building looking down at the city from a hilltop. It seemed to me filled more with people who appeared in the society pages of the newspaper than with art. But, at the Good Fairy's insistence, I went to Philadelphia for an interview. I'm climbing up the rows and rows of steps to the entrance of the Museum, and thinking that becoming a part of this place is highly improbable. But up the forever steps I walk, focusing on my breathing, and into the Director's Office, where a large, cultivated presence receives me with,

"You know you're a dark horse in this race."

He shouldn't have said that. It hit me wrong, and I shot back, "You know, *you're* a dark horse in *this* race as well."

We stood looking at one another - and then that man broke into laughter. Don't you know I got the job. I assumed the position of Chief of the Division of Education at the Philadelphia Museum of Art on a cold January 7, 1977, walked back up those long steps - and went to work for ten years.

MANSARDS AND MANDAPAMS

"Krishnamurti's on the phone. She wants to talk to you."

"I'm on the *other* phone."

It's my first week at the Philadelphia Museum of Art, as Chief of the Division of Education, and the phones never stop ringing.

"She has some questions about the mandapam. She's calling from India."

"*Mandapam?* It's made from sesame seeds and I don't like it. Why don't *you* talk to her?" I tell my secretary.

"She wants to talk to *you*."

"Why does she want to know about mandapam?"

"*Pick it up, Ted.*"

"In a minute. Listen, Mom, some lady from India's calling me about food. Remember I used to pick up mandapam at the deli for Gram?"

"Back then we called it *marzipan*," Mom says.

"Whatever. I've gotta go. Why don't you call someone else?"

"*They* don't work in a museum," she says.

"I gotta go, Mom."

"Hello, Krishnamurti. How are *you?*"

Krishnamurti is fine, a mandapam is a porch-like structure leading to a temple, we have one in the Museum, and she's coming to dance in it. Good. Yes. Wonderful. The closest *I've* come to a temple is combing my hair but that's gonna change now.

Later, Mom says "The woman's nuts to come all the way from India just to do a little dance in that thing. What's it gonna cost to get her here?" Mom won't make a long-distance phone call without a clock in front of her, and is still talking about the Great Depression.

The next day the phones start ringing again. "Meredith Savory's on the phone. She wants to talk to you."

Savory? Maybe *she* wants a recipe for salad dressing.

"Hello, I'm from the Philadelphia Cultural Alliance. We represent the museums in the area and, since *you* represent the Art Museum, we hope you will be a presenter at our program - *Philadelphia Homes: A Look Inside* - to be held at several neighborhood centers. We're reaching out."

Right now you're reaching *wrong* because I know zero about architecture *anywhere*. But I'm not going to tell *her* that, and I haven't been at the Museum long enough to figure out what I *do* know. Most of me is still in the Blue Ridge Mountains, working out ways to bring art and people closer together. So earlier today, I'm walking through the Museum's Decorative Arts collection thinking, *I'd* call that sofa a turbulent cadenza, that big ornate desk, a bravo stupendum, and that tiny chair, a weeny - defecto - supposo. A cat couldn't fit in it! Now, folks, what names can *you* come up with? What do *the rest of us* think they look like? And then let's find out why some people call them something else. It helps me to laugh when I don't know what to do next. Sometimes it gets me started. But enough - Meredith Savory's on the phone.

"You can imagine how busy I am right now, being new on the job," I tell her.

"I *can* imagine," she pushes back, "but *we want* you to be a part of this program. I'm sure *you* could just show up and talk."

Don't count on it. *We want!* But I can see where this is going - and she bags me. I figure I'll throw something together. How much can folks at a neighborhood center know about the architecture of Philadelphia homes?

"Sure, I'll be glad to do it," I lie.

Soon the time is approaching for me to show at the neighborhood center. I skim through a couple books on Philadelphia architecture but can't get into it. Never could - which is why I left Philadelphia after high school. I'm gonna have to wing it. It's not easy to talk a lot about something you know nothing about but people do it all the time. I've done it myself - so maybe I can talk the audience into believing there's a rabbit in the hat. There's the phone again! And it's the *savory* one.

"You might like to hear one of the other speakers, at *his* neighborhood center, before you give *your* talk next week. Bill Cornerstone is speaking tomorrow night. You probably already know one another - Bill is the president of the Philadelphia Historical Society. Blah. Blah."

"Thanks for calling," I reply, "I'll get over there."

The place is packed when I arrive, and a picture of a roof is projected onto a big screen. Bill Cornerstone has white hair and *looks* like he knows whatever he's talking about. Sometimes that's a big part of it. He's talking about *mansards,* and it turns out I do know something about those birds. I've seen them before at a zoo - ducks from China, with a crest of feathers on top of their heads. So what do Chinese ducks have to do with rooftops? The answer is nothing - unless they're sitting on them. And, anyway, I remember that the ducks I saw were *mandarins.* There's no way I can do this next week! I've got the *hat* - but there's no rabbit in it. Or, more worrisome, there's a *dead* rabbit in it. And dead rabbits don't hop. I'm in trouble. Mom calls later that night with her usual opener, "So what's cookin'?" and I tell her my rabbit problem.

"So what!" she says. "I know a lot of rabbits that look dead but there are ways to wake 'em up."

"That's not helping me, Mom!"

But guess what? The very next day, I'm having lunch in the Museum cafeteria and overhear someone talking about growing up on a rabbit farm in France.

"Eet was deefficult for me to geeve up my pet bonnies when zee time came."

"It must have been *terrible*," I threw in, and moved a seat closer to her, grieving over those bunnies until we were alone at the table.

"I'm Madelaine Belmain," she says.

Belmain? Loosely translated that means a *good hand.* A sign - and I tell her *my* sad rabbit story.

"You 'ave no more problem," she cried, "I majored in art 'istory weez a concentration in architecture. I weel 'elp you. I make you a rabbit! "

And did she ever! A week later we *hit* the Northeast Neighborhood Center. Well, rather Madelaine did, wearing the greatest hat I'd ever seen. She was more *French* than a movie with subtitles - and, like I said, sometimes that's a big part of it. And as if that weren't enough, it sounded to me like she knew more than Bill Cornerstone - although I think she could have talked about canning apricots and blown away that crowd. She took over, the talk went well, everyone went home, and I remained at the Museum for another ten years of phone calls. Not only that. I know what a mansard is. Madelaine became my lifelong friend. And Meredith Savory moved to Oregon.

TEN THOUSAND SHADES OF WHITE

"Miss Lee just called and wants to know if you're free to come by her office." my secretary says.

This is it, I tell myself, and start to wet my shirt. I've been on the job as Chief of the Division of Education at the Philadelphia Museum of Art for less than a month, still pining for the mountains of North Carolina, and certain that I know nothing about nothing. *Why would Miss Lee want to see me?* I ask the sky between the bars on my office window.

But first. During the weekly curator's meeting - another wet shirt - while the Museum director was tormenting a curator, my bolting eyes crashed into those of Miss Lee. I assumed that was the end of it, when the meeting was over, and got out of there fast.

Miss Lee, by the way, is Curator of Far Eastern Art, a venerable figure, feared by some at the Museum but greatly liked by the guards and maintenance staff. That might have told me something I had yet to discover. Still, I had heard someone call her The Wicked Witch of the East and decided to give her wide berth. It was said that her infallible "*eye*" could determine 10,000 shades of white. I know zero about Chinese painting, and for me, white is white. Why does she want to see me?

"Tell Miss Lee I'm in conference."

My secretary, a veteran of the Museum, tells me to go as summoned. "Just pay the ticket, Ted."

The door to Miss Lee's office is already open. It seems wider than most doors. A sea of people comes into view. Miss Lee rises like an iceberg and turns toward me. I'm going to hit it.

"Dr. Katz," the Witch says, cordially.

"Miss Lee," I reply, cordially.

Crash! I've done it again!

"Come join us," she says, directing me to a long table, draped with black cloth, upon which lay what appear to be chunks of ice.

126

My ship is going to go down.

"I know nothing about Asian art," I try, groping for a life jacket.

That doesn't stop her. She introduces me to the *art specialists* from New York, circling the room like sharks.

"This is *not* my field. I'm *not* familiar with Chinese art," I counter.

But she's got me and holding. *Not! Not!* Is she deaf?

"We believe one of the two pieces of white jade on the table was done by a master of the period; the other was not. What do you think?"

What do I think about what! I'm dead.

"I doubt that I can contribute anything to this scrutiny," I parry, pleased with the word *scrutiny*.

"Look at them," she blocks, crushing my escape.

There's no place to go but toward that dreadful jade. *Why are you doing this?*

"Look at them," she repeats, gently.

"It's hard to say."

"*Look at them.*"

I'm sorry I looked at *her* that day. I'm going down, recalling fairy tales in which nice people have their heads lopped off because they don't have answers to questions. I crane my head stiffly over the table, intending to give the impression that I can't see the objects clearly. The Witch doesn't miss it.

"You may pick them up and look more closely at them," she proposes, and hands me a pair of white cotton gloves. I put the gloves on, consider lunging for her throat, and instead reach for a piece of jade. The carving is ornate and highly polished – impressive and pretty. It must have required great skill. Easy enough, I decide, put it back, and pick up the other piece of jade. *What's this!* It looks like it was hacked out with an ice pick. The surfaces are rough, and there are deep chisel marks left in it. It looks coarse to me. I don't see the issue. Meanwhile Miss Lee is going on, *"Look at it."*

I *am* looking. *How long do I have to look* before telling her what has to be clear to all of us, and walking out of here with my head attached? But every time I open my mouth, she jumps in with, "Look at it!" And then, a surprising thing happens. The room, the New Yorkers, and Miss Lee vanish - and I'm alone with the jade carving - *feeling* it.

"Look at it," Miss Lee is saying from wherever she is. *See* the strength in the second carving that is lacking in the first. *See* that the forceful chisel marks feel authoritative, indicating that the artist means for them to remain there. *See* that, when compared to the second piece, the first is a technical achievement lacking emotional power.

From my mouth sprang, "I believe the second carving is that of the master."

"Thank you," she says. "That's our conclusion as well."

And so began one of the great friendships of my life. Miss Lee is gone but hardly a day goes by when I don't hear her urging, "*Look at it.*" And who knows? One day I may even see ten thousand shades of white.

TRAVELING DAYS

"Ask questions from the heart and you will be answered from the heart." - Omaha

IT'S NOT REAL

"When I was about fifteen, I auditioned for the Ballet Russe de Monte Carlo. [The choreographer] called us one by one. When my turn came there was a hush in that place like you wouldn't believe. I was the only little black face around... [The choreographer] told me, "The only trouble is, in order for you to belong to the company, I would have to paint you white. You wouldn't like that, would you?" I said, "No, I wouldn't want that." So I thanked him and went out...and I...cried."
- Janet Collins

In the summer of 1962, I up and walk out of dental school - and take a train to Colorado College to study dance. The ballerina, Janet Collins is dancing at The Broadmoor International Theater. Maybe I'll get to meet her, I think. Well, no sooner do I check into my dormitory room, when I'm standing in the dinner line in the College cafeteria, listening to all these dance students going on about how someone saw Janet Collins coming this way and - whoosh! - a bright green cape wings into the room like a flying emerald.

"It's Janet Collins," someone squeals.

"Look! Janet Collins."

The next thing I know, she's right behind me in line. I've never seen anyone like that in my life - at least not close up. I can't take my eyes off of the colossal globe of hair that sits like a monument on top of her head.

And that radiant woman looks at me and says, "Hello."

I'm staring at her head, and she is looking right into my eyes, and smiling.

And I come out with, "Your *hair* is incredible" - and I'm not even finished, when up go her hands, and she pops that article right off her head and hands it to me.

"It's not real," she says.

I'm standing there holding the thing, staring at the spot where it had just been, and wondering how she was going to stick it back on again. She's holding me by the eyes, and laughing, "It's not real. It *isn't* real."

Then she snatches it from me, drops it into her shoulder bag, and turns to talk to someone. Later at night in my room, I can't remember anything else about the day. And that's how I first came to know Janet Collins. Today, almost fifty years later, I can still hear her loud and clear, "It's not real."

Janet and I talked all summer - about everything, from the shapes of clouds to how a dancer moves across the floor and lots of others things as well. I hadn't thought much before about what is real but I think it had a lot to do with why I walked out of dental school. Janet must have seen that in the dinner line when her eyes got hold of mine. One day, we went walking in The Garden of the Gods, a suggestive rock formation near the school, and she talked about what *was* real.

"What do you think I did the night I won the Donaldson Award for best female dancer in a Broadway show? I went back to my apartment, filled a bucket with soapy water, got down on the floor and scrubbed it clean. I wanted to remind myself of what is real."

What could I say? I didn't know then how much scrubbing lay ahead of me but I expect she did. She went on to tell me that, when she danced with the Metropolitan Opera, she refused to wear a white body stocking, and

Rudolph Bing, General Manager of the Opera, allowed her to go on stage without the camouflage.

"The Met had never seen a black face," she recalled. "Marian Anderson couldn't get in there. I felt like a doorknob. I was the dancer that opened the door."

But there was more.

"The Metropolitan Opera was going on tour. Mr. Bing called me into his office one day and he was very uncomfortable. He said, 'Miss Collins, I do not like what I have to tell you, but I am not Abraham Lincoln.' He said he could not take me south on tour because there was a law down there that blacks and whites could not appear on the same stage together."

Janet got me thinking hard about *what* is real.

I learned that summer that leaving a life that was not real was a good start but *becoming* real was a long way off. Janet was the first of many doorknobs I would meet. While I thought I was studying dance, I was closing and opening doors, finding out what mattered to me - and what didn't. Janet Collins taught me to reach.

WIZARD OF WALNUT COVE

Tom phones to tell me that my clay pot has been fired and is ready to be picked up.

"How did it come out?"

"It looks good," Tom says.

I've taken a job in North Carolina to teach English. Looking for a way to meet new friends, I joined a clay workshop and found myself strangling a wad of red squish. My fight with the clay got resolved as a squatting troll. Tom suggested it might make a nice cookie jar. Pleased, I painted it in bright pastel colors and left it to be fired. Today I am going to get it.

"I've come for my cookie jar," I tell Tom, who is holding a large petrified turd.

"You're looking at it."

"What happened to the color?"

"It changes in the firing."

Tom considers the dreadful lump and has the sauce to tell me, "The color looks good."

"*What* color?"

I take the thing and go home.

That's how I came to meet Tom. Although, I decided to drop ceramics, I carried that thing with me for years, telling people it was a meteorite. One day, it just upped and disappeared. But it really had come from a faraway place, as, I thought, did Tom, who had come from Minnesota to North Carolina to teach ceramics. Gypsy, a local weaver, offered him an acre of her land on which to build a house and settle. That's just what Tom did. The house sits in the woods off of Piney Mountain Road in Walnut Cove. Early on it had no plumbing or electricity. But it had a sauna and tall pines to keep the sky up.

The first time I drove out to Walnut Cove with Tom, he stopped his truck on an empty stretch of road.

"What're we stopping for," I asked.

"There's a turtle in the road."

Where I come from, people don't stop for turtles. But to be honest, we didn't have turtles. So we sat in nothing nowhere and waited for that turtle to finish walking. And that's when I *saw* the red clay fields and the tobacco-colored barns that were to stay with me from that day forward.

TOM'S COUNTRY

Walnut Cove, North Carolina. September, 1968

"Soft rain," Gypsy said, "It bends the leaves back."

She told us that life goes quickly, and I saw John watch her look off into the pines. Susan said that the Bay tree had grown, and Gypsy knew she was an old woman.

We are like old times in Tom's country - walking in the night, quiet until the teapot calls us to the kitchen, back to being quiet again. The clouds are changing - that was the first I noticed it. Mornings are cold. September comes like June came - a caress, a sense of it.

Susan said, "The horses got out last night so I went out to put them up. Then I sat late on the back porch to watch the wind blow the clouds across the moon."

I said I thought the moon held a lot of water, that the night felt swollen.

"Like March," she whispered.

Wanda gave me a yellow mountain to paint, and when we hugged one another there was a kind of holding on before another time began.

When I left Walnut Cove it was raining. John was rubbing a leaf in his hands, and there was a fly in the room.

Gypsy said, "Well come and stay."

As I drove away I watched their arms in the rearview mirror turn to waving grass. During the night the car and I broke down in Virginia, on 85 North. I pulled off the road, put a sign on the window, HELP, curled up with the thunder of trucks, and waited.

CADMIUM RED

Off of Piney Mountain Road, about a quarter of a mile through the woods, is a two acre clearing which is Susan's piece of land. On it stands a small stable which housed the horse that Susan bought from a woman in Virginia and which turned out to be lame. The horse's leg had been shot full of cortisone or something which made it seem to be okay and when Susan got the horse home the stuff wore off and it limped. Susan didn't take the horse back because she didn't want to hurt the woman's feelings and figured if she hadn't bought it somebody else would have or it would have been shot. Later, in a bad trade she lost the horse and wound up with nothing. The stable is empty and the door lies open banging against the barn in the wind.

Susan Thomas was once my wildly restless red-haired friend. She loved her green satin dress, her black stockings and her cadmium red shoes, as did I. Gypsy gave Susan Thomas Young an isolated piece of land on which to build a house and raise her baby. The one-room house looks down through still trees onto a dark pond. It is painted red and has a tin roof for listening to the rain. It has a portable heater next to a crib, a painting of a tall tree in orange foliage on a plywood divider between the toilet and the washer and drier, bowls of dusty field flowers, a saddle, a radio, a photograph of a red-haired baby, a panda bear, a double bed with one pillow, a Sweet Sixteen Donuts bag with three left and a ten pound bag of Purina Cat Chow.

There are, in that room, two posters:

BLOOM WHERE YOU ARE PLANTED

IF THERE IS NO WIND - ROW

And, pasted on a piece of white muslin, a page of faded wide-lined school paper on which is carefully printed in pencil:

GOD BLESS MISS THOMAS

Pinned to the inside of the door is a card with yellow flowers painted around the edges:

In appreciation.

Our lives are surely much richer

since we have come to know you.

And a poem written by Susan, Sunday morning, November 16, 1975:

Those withering ones who've bloomed their days away,

Look at them nodding and blowing

without understanding,

Dryly, softly, gently

sowing their life on the wind.

And a postcard from John, PM Nov., 1964, with a poem by S.T. Coleridge:

"If a man could pass through Paradise in a dream,

and have a flower presented to him as a pledge

that his soul had really been there, and if he

found that flower in his hand when he awoke -

Ay! and what then?"

The motto of North Carolina is ESSE QUAM VIDERI, which means to be rather than to seem.

OZARK CATFISH

Eureka Springs, Arkansas, 1975

I'm leaving today.

The snow that began to fall last night has been coming down heavily all day. Through the restaurant window, between the letters of OZARK CATFISH, Spring Street looks pretty like the ones in my picture books when I was a child on a sick-at-home day.

Up the hill and around the corner - Jerome in front and Edward in back - carrying Christmas packages, each alongside a lady with skinny legs. Jim the Drug Store, pulls the chains, tink! tink!, flips the sign, CLOSED, walks slowly up the hill - and down the hill slowly comes the tan pickup. Merry Christmas, slowly street. In your streets and people I've found quiet.

I've been to the Girlie Show at the County Fair, been over sixteen and broadminded, and roared with the crowd for Miss Kitty from Kansas City, and the Foreign Girl from Winnipeg, Canada. I saw for myself "From the Island of Katabi – feets like a monkey, eyes like a chicken. Alive!" I carried the bumper stickers, "All of Satan's apples have worms," "God has the hairs on your head numbered – and on your wig, too," and, "The King is Coming."

I'm leaving today, carrying within me a town where people know one another by their trucks - and where that's pretty much all they need to know. Ken says, "You'll be back." But I may be taking what I pretty much need to know with me.

IN A CHINESE RESTAURANT

Cambridge, Massachusetts, 1976

Sometimes one *knows* things long before they have fully taken hold of one. Like the man who can tell you, under a blue sky, that rain is coming.

"Something in the air," he said. "You can *feel* it."

That's how I *knew* in a Chinese restaurant that we were done with one another.

You rub your fingers on the table top, then, self-consciously stop. You smoke a cigarette and put it out, rubbing the bottom of the ashtray until it seems too long.

I'm uncomfortable now, sitting across the table from you, and look to distance myself by thinking about other times we spent together. The bright summer we went beach-combing near Seattle, when, reaching in the sand for stones and shells, I found the blue agates in your eyes.

I puff out my cheeks and make a cave. The warm tea lies quietly beneath my tongue. I sail boats in and out.

In New Mexico, I thought of us as undertow and taste of salt, wave hollow and foam, earth swell and field flower, rapid and leaf. Goodnight, I prayed, and blinded myself with you.

You chew ice.

Things were different in Monett, Missouri. It was a cold winter. And you're right - don't drive in bad weather. Get to a motel and stay put. Inside our room, the radiator coughs and bangs, a train's keening screws the night to the walls and hoarse trucks splinter the dark.

I watch the cashier and the rain outside.

The window over Third Avenue in New York City pounds in the wind like the Salvation Army this morning near Wall Street. My silence scrapes itself along the sides of buildings and crawls back into my chest. Your head protrudes from its serape tube like the top of a worm and grinds its teeth. Dogs in the city sound different from dogs in the country.

You push crumbs from the table with your index finger.

Asheville, North Carolina. The wonderful house and garden. We're burning out.

I look at other people to see what they do when they sit together.

The dreams are twinkled out - used up. We've become weary. No more, I tell myself quietly.

You crack your teeth the way you do sometimes in your sleep.

Back in my Chevy, time is not an explanation but movement - a highway to slide into - darting light, dumb platelet - particular energy, randomly conforming. I allow that it suits me. Chevybelly dark I call it - homecoming.

SILVER CREEK

Hutchinson, Kansas, July 3, 1975

It's 11 p.m. and I'm moving out and on, once again. Silver Creek remains in the bedroom with the things I'm leaving behind.

The day of the River Quay Art Show, the wind was blowing and my matted drawings sailed off the table top and into the street. I found Silver Creek in a vacant lot, filled it with my pictures and carried it every weekend to the art fairs. Together we did Topeka, Antioch, Prairie Village, and all the other fairs that year. That wooden crate with its bright red letters held my pictures and comforted me. It sometimes seemed Silver Creek was my partner in life. I came to love that little crate and, on leaving it, felt maybe it had come to love me back.

When I say good-bye tonight to Silver Creek, we are both empty. The pictures are gone. Funny, what we come to love, and what seems to love us back. My hardest good-byes have been to rooms, trees, chairs – and a crate called Silver Creek.

INDIAN SPRINGS

Indian Springs, Kansas, May 9, 1975

Since early this morning I've been sitting with my drawings at an art fair in a shopping mall, in Indian Springs, Kansas, staring into the eyes of *Betty Oliver*. Spirited Betty Oliver, stuck on a pegboard, a long way from the mountains of North Carolina. Together, we wait hopefully for customers - obstructions between The Rib Shack and Don's World of Beef.

Complaining that my spotlights are blinding them, a couple walk past my pictures and join the crowd at the Wurlitzer store singing *Getting to Know You*. Betty says nothing. She thinks it doesn't matter.

Roberta, the next artist over, leaves her paintings of red tornadoes full of arms trying to get out, and comes over to smoke a cigarette. She tells me she won a contest for floating and her new husband turns her on.

Noticing that I've sold nothing, she says, "You'll learn to take the bitter with the sweet."

Betty says, "Let it go, Ted."

Roberta offers, "Why don't you go grab a Hot Sam and Peach Julius? I'll keep an eye on your work."

When I return, Betty Oliver is off the pegboard.

"This landscape was more colorful," Roberta suggests, and asks, "How do you look in a bathing suit?"

"I don't know. I just swim in them."

I stick Betty back on the pegboard and ask Roberta why she paints red tornadoes. She tells me she went down a sliding board at a public swimming pool and her bathing suit came *entirely* off at the top while she shot to the bottom.

"But tornadoes are terrible. The other day I saw one in my backyard."

Lowering her voice, she adds, "Some man looked at your work for a long time while you were gone. He went through all the pictures in the orange crate and read everything. He was even going to look at your sketchbook but I gave him a dirty look and he went away. He was a colored boy." Betty Oliver gazes wearily at Roberta.

Some art show judges come by with lots of ribbons, complaining that it took them forever to make a decision, and hand me one. Roberta races over right away. She's never won anything in her life, she says, hanging my ribbon where everyone will see it because it's good for business. She adds that she's reducing the prices of her tornadoes fifty percent.

A man stops to look at my paintings and tells me he does stuff just like them but didn't win anything for them. Betty winks. One hour to go.

"I like *this*!" a voice exclaims, pointing to the palette on which I've placed a stack of name cards encircled by gobs of moist paint. I wonder how much I could get for it. When people ask about my blue tablecloth, I send them to Venture's. One woman went nuts over my pot filled with fresh flowers, and wanted to know how I made them look so real. I told her I didn't - God did - and she walked away stewed.

At one of these art shows, I brought along a big bath towel with an American Indian pattern, to cover my table with. There was a nasty draft in that mall and someone told me she had my space two years ago and got pneumonia. I figured I needed that towel more than the table did, and wrapped myself up in it. Right away, a man approaches and asks me gently what tribe I'm from. So I told him, The Bath Towel tribe. He got mad as hell. But wait - once, at an outdoor show, someone wanted to buy my dog.

"Isn't that cute?" a child comments, as she walks by my palette with her father.

"Very nice," he replies.

"Hey mister, how about a picture of a lake with a fish poking its head out!"

Betty frowns. You're out of line, Ted.

Meanwhile, all day, people are jabbing their fingers in the wet paint on my palette. The favorite color is red - and damn it - some kid's poked his hand in the paint and is reaching for the underside of the blue tablecloth.

"Hey, get your hands outta there. *Not on my blue tablecloth!*"

"How'm I gonna get it off?"

Then, an announcement that the artists can go home now - the fair is over. Roberta squints. Betty blinks. And I gather up the blue tablecloth to wrap my pictures in. *Goddamn them!* Red paint along the whole underside!

Roberta's already helping the man who paints bulls pack his pictures. She's telling him she likes bulls, and she sold over seven hundred caramel apples one day.

"I stood up and told 'em they could eat 'em with dentures!"

Goodnight, Roberta.

Outside smells of grass, and the taste of freedom is strong in my mouth. Being an artist suits me. Betty Oliver takes off her hat, and we head for Kansas City.

ROBERT TELLS

Wichita, Kansas, September 2, 1974

"It's pretty out here," I said to a man on a fence. "Feels like a change of season in the air."

"Well, yes," he answered, looking out, "There's some things to tell about the seasons."

"Myself, I'm just passing through," I let him know.

"Cooler in the evenin's now. That turn the trees yellow. I don't care what tree you look at will be a solid gold color. When the trees are gold, wind gone blow. Yards be covered with leaves. Trees are naked. Pretty soon the snow gone start flyin'. You wake up in the mornin' and trees are bent to the ground. Cedar tree - you know how they bush up? They be all out and bent over. They go back up again later. You could step right outside right now – there's not one thing that not covered by ice. It's beautiful. It looks like a dingy dream but it's real. I've seen pictures like it on television. Well, maybe if the wind blowin' hard, the ice on the limbs hits each other and they make a noise like these wooden charms – these Japanese things. Kind of a hollow sound. They'll bang and clang! You can just go up to one of them trees and cover your head and grab hold of a limb that's hangin' down and shake 'em like heck."

"Snow. The beauty is the same as ice, except it's only snow. There's no noise. When snow falls it's more or less a silent thing. You don't really hear it too much. About six months of winter. After awhile you get tired of seein' 'em this way. You know, no grass – just the evergreens and the winter grass stays green. Then the trees start gettin' thick. You know, they're thin all winter. They get covered with thousands of buds. Flowers that die in the winter and bloom in the spring starts comin' up. What you think are dead will green back up. Beautiful. I don't see how it does it. Then everything is burnt up by the heat. Now in those months, the hotter the temperature the more things'll turn brown. Severe weather. Hailstones can get the size of grapefruits, which they've been reported right here. It's different every year. I don't care how much you see it, every year it's different. It's beauty."

"What're you writin' all that down for?"

"It's poetic."

"It's *what?*"

"Poetic."

"Well, you'll *see* it if you stay."

ROBERT TALKS

Wichita, Kansas, September 1, 1974

"Ever see a tornado?" I asked him.

"Yessir," he said, shaping a little hill of dirt with the toe of his boot.

"They ain't one cloud outta line, they just so perfect down in the tunnel. You cain't see 'em at night, only by lightnin'. You can hear 'em, 'cause it's so quiet when it comes you won't hear a bird chirpin'. Then it sounds like a hunnert freight trains comin'. It does. The closer it gets, the louder the roar gets but it don't honk. You know how a freight train will honk for a crossin'?"

"Like I say, it can take, I'm not lyin' – this happened back at home – six hours for a storm to build up. Dad got home about 5:30. It was bad lookin'. The clouds got green. When you live in a storm area you can tell what it gone do, pretty near. Dad and me watched the storm. Mom started gettin' dinner ready. Supper – put it that way."

"Soon as the sireens blew we jumped up from the table. This is the way it happened. We grabbed the flashlights and headed two houses down south to the shelter. We got halfway between our house and the shelter. It just suddenly quit everything. It was rainin' down hard, water over your shoetop, like this, and suddenly it quit. You know the way a faucet will be runnin' and you shut it off? There just ain't no rain." Have you ever been scared? You feel real light in your stomach. It's rainin' like a motherfucker and zap it stops! There ain't no sound at all. There is nothing - just the roar. We could hear it comin'."

"Back in Kansas you watch animals. They'll never lie to you. This is no lie. Bird'll eat heavy before a storm. Squirrels'll tell you when your first snow's comin'. Clouds'll tell you. And red lightning means hail."

Talking squirrels and red lightning.

BANJO AND FIDDLE

Santa Fe, New Mexico, August, 1975

Mr. Pacheco and Mr. Vigil came down from the mountains of Truchas to the rodeo fairgrounds to compete in the Spanish Fiddle Contest. They're the only contestants and win the Grand Prize. Mr. Pacheco accepts the winner's cup for the pair and, encouraged by the howling crowd, proceeds to sing. Mr. Vigil shrugs, and walks away. The mistress of ceremonies looks at her watch, Mr. Pacheco is removed from the stage, and the other contests get going.

Contestants are allowed a warm-up tune and two contest pieces; three judges swill beer and wave the performers on - and off - the stage. The scheduled performances end but the wily performers reshuffle with frenzied excitement and return to the stage as new groups. Following Mr. Pacheco's lead, the spirited contestants, buoyed by the crowd, the beer, and one another, are not wanting to give up the stage.

"Who was that? They're not listed in the program."

"Was that the warm-up or the contest piece?"

"We just heard you!"

163

"No. *She* wasn't in it! They were the Mason's Apron. We're Fiddle 'n' Pick!"

"Can you guys do Orange Blossom Special?"

"Fraid not but next year we will."

"Emergency announcement! We need three beers for the judges. Concession is out! Anybody have 'em? There's gonna be a Grand Finale to this contest so don't be in a rush to leave and – yo! - more beer has been found!"

The mistress of ceremonies punches the air with her fists, the mob roars, and The Instant Women's Journey refuses to leave the stage.

"Get off already!"

"You just played that!"

"Next!!!"

Heading home out of the fairgrounds, my rear-view mirror and I fill up with the big darkness of another New Mexico night.

AS LONG AS A WINTER'S NIGHT

Lewisville, North Carolina, February, 1976

Some folks have come from as far away as Opp, Alabama and Century, Florida to the sale of M.C. Benton's dairy herd, "the largest in the county," at Brook Acre Farm.

Evening is coming on and only a few animals are still waiting to get sold.

"At five-hundred eighty-five! She's as long as a winter's night, and every inch of her is a dairy cow. Who'll give me six hundred?"

Confined by farmers, a yellow cow looks out at the lean man in a Dixie Fertilizer cap. He spits and softly nods.

"Sold for six seventy-five!"

The Lewisville Jaycees thread in and out of the farmers, drawing them closer together.

"Hot dogs! Fries!"

"She made nine-hundred dollars over feed costs, and she's a-milkin' real good. Take a look! Take a look! She's a promising young thing. She's a-mikin' sixty-four pounds a day. Who'll give me five-hundred dollars? We'll be out of here by milking time."

This small red cow stands quietly eyeing the trailers waiting like dark pumpkins in the pastures of Brook Acre Farm, and I wonder if she, too, feels from somewhere a brown dumbness arrive.

"Last chance!" the Jaycees call.

MR. E.M. BLEVINS

Jefferson, North Carolina, March, Thursday, 1976

Mr. E. M. Blevins and his homemade banjo stopped by today to talk for awhile. He was a shy man, and told me he was retired. We shook hands, and it came as no surprise to learn that his kind of banjo picking is called claw hammer. He asked me what songs I knew, and told me the names of the songs he knew. We talked and passed the banjo back and forth like a peace pipe.

He said the songs I knew were good songs to know.

He said I ought to come and get together with him and his friends, and pick some of the old tunes.

He said I was welcome in Jefferson.

We sang away the afternoon, and when it got dark, Mr. E. M. Blevins went home. The mountain smelled strong that night.

AN OFFAL TIME

Edinburgh, Fall, 1994

It's raining tonight in Edinburgh. A Scottish Evening at a nearby hotel sounds good but as soon as I walk into that place I figure I've been had. Corralled along with the other captives, I receive a *traditional drink* - a paper cupful of something that could have seeped up out of a graveyard - and driven forward between two bagpipers, into a big room, where we're set like pins at long tables - and the doors are shut. There's no way out. I apologize to the rain. You didn't need to do *this*!

There's no time to think. I'm looking for something to dump the drink into, when we're assaulted by a comet shower of serving maids. Our Scottish meal will begin with turnips, potatoes, and haggis. Haggis? Turnips and potatoes I know - *haggis* I don't, and the Irish tourists at my table are talking about whether to eat it – or not. That's enough for me. As a man for whom yogurt is an adventure, I figure I'd better flag one of those comets and find out more about the haggis.

"What's in it?"

"It's awful," she says.

"I know – that's what I'm hearing. But what's in it?"

She looks away. "I don't eat it. It's awful."

Awful? I'm thinking - maybe it's shit! People eat all kinds of things.

"Hold the haggis and make the potatoes a double."

All the Irish pins at my table turn toward me.

"I like potatoes."

"She's trying to tell you that haggis is *offal* - a pudding of heart, liver and lungs, boiled in the stomach of the animal."

"Yeah, well I really *do* like potatoes."

Bad enough but it turns out that *most* awful comes *after* supper - a horror of song and dance performed by children who should be sleeping. Rain never felt so good, when I finally got out of that place. Hopefully, the fifty bucks I gave goes into a retirement fund for those kids.

THE BLUE HOUR

Paris, 1994

"Last year's words belong to last year's language; and next year's words await another voice." - T.S.Eliot

An apse is not a dangerous snake and reliquaries are not estate jewelry. The guide book is useful. It suggests that I might discover thousands of figures inside the Chapel of Sainte-Chapelle. Right away I can see at least a thousand of them - and with cameras. That's was easy. I thread around until I've seen enough and swim out of there into the wind and sunlight to play with hats and shoes and dogs. Paris, after-all, is *outside*.

Humming about, I join an *enthusiasm* of hats and shoes pouring into a hole in the ground like so much sand in an hourglass, and end up in the tummy of the Louvre. The thousand figures with cameras got there first - and are charging Mona Lisa.

"Oh my God!" someone gasps.

"It's Mona Lisa!"

Mona is smiling amiably behind a sign: NO FLASHBULBS.

Pop! A bulb goes off.

Pop! Pop! The cameras fire at Mona.

Pop! Pop! Pop!

Mona winces.

When the firing lets up, the thousand figures will undoubtedly want to salt and butter her. I'll come back.

It's the *blue hour*, and in that lonesome heartbeat between day and night, I find a bench in the Tuileries and curl up in air the color of Gram's wool coat.

Blink! - Gram and l'heure bleu are gone. Paris is done for the day.

LONELY DRUG LORD

Ranchos de Taos, New Mexico, September, 1986

"The neighbors are talking. They think you're a drug lord. Not a user or a dealer - a lord!"

My landlady, Sophia, has stopped by. Since I came here to become somebody else, why not a drug lord! When Sophia leaves, I get to a mirror and try out some expressions. I suppose I could look like a drug lord. I've got the Lincoln Town Car parked outside my trailer, the closed curtains, and the people in and out day and night. Maybe someone saw the cop come to my door - one of the first responses to my notice.

I told him, "Just put the gun on the table, next to your clothes."

Summer was done, and September was rotting from yellow to slate. It does that in Ranchos de Taos, New Mexico. Summer was gone, and figuring the locals would miss the income tourists provided, I put an ad in the paper: "Artist seeks models. Good pay." The phone never stopped ringing. People showed up in every shape and color - and I began to paint. Three models a day, three hours a session: in at nine, out at noon; in at one, out at four; in at seven, out at ten. In and out they went - like pendulums. The windows stayed covered up except when I checked the weather.

I had come here to test myself. It was a decision that arrived one day and wouldn't leave - the kind friends say takes courage. But there wasn't any courage to it. There was no other choice left. It was the last tag! If it didn't work, I would let it go. Being a drug lord struck me as an interesting alternative. So when I wasn't painting, or swimming laps at the community center, I drove the Lincoln around - just in case. And what was I doing anyway with a brand new Lincoln Town Car? Here's what - a rental car company in Portland, Oregon, offered me an absurdly low rate for a two month rental and I took it, tossed my art supplies and a radio into one of those big cars and left for New Mexico. Weeks passed, models came and went, paintings piled up, trees shed their leaves, cold got bad, and streets got empty. Sleep came and went, like the models. I learned to know the different grays of night - four o'clock, a blue gray; five o'clock, a pink gray.

In time, I turned off the radio and listened to the sounds of birds, horses and children in the fields behind the house. *Out of the blue*, Mom and Dad dropped by one day to visit. They said they were just out taking a drive - *from Philadelphia?* It struck me as odd that they would up and go for a two thousand mile drive but I was glad to see them. They hit and ran - no tears, no counseling. A meal together and off they went like little blessings. And in came the next model.

That fall I learned to not feel lonely, and it happened in surprising ways. I began to enjoy doing nothing, and finding that nothing is sometimes something. I watched out the kitchen window the farmers driving their old trucks, and Sophia's stallion snorting the wind. I watched the Spanish kids in the restaurant, hugging and laughing to the songs of Freddy Fender, when they weren't cooking or serving customers. I bought a tape of Freddy Fender and stopped listening to Chopin. I ate alone at The

Garden Restaurant, and stayed late, along with one or two others, to listen to an old man play guitar. Alone, I swam at the community center, listened to the sounds of dogs barking at night, smelled chili cooking, and saw the days changing color. Somewhere in all that, I forgot to be lonely.

And then something happened. I woke up one day before dawn, took down the shower curtain that covered the kitchen window, and looked out into the night. Startled, I could barely make out scores of huge dark discs hanging over the field behind the trailer - and they were glowing on their bottoms. My heart began to hammer. An invasion! And I'm the only one awake. Russians! No - space-ships with little fires underneath! Interesting - so that's how they fly. I wonder if our people know that. Aliens landing in the field behind my house! Too scary - blink! blink! blink!. They're still out there, hovering, silent dark things with those little glowy spots on them. Too many models! Too much alone! I've cracked! I don't like this dream - blink! blink! blink! Wake up! I'm sweating. There's no time. What to do? I'll need a weapon. I look around the kitchen. The best I can find is a fork or a paint brush.

The morning light is coming up behind the mountains and the discs are now spheres. I wonder how many *things* are on those things? Should I hide or surrender? The light outside is growing brighter. The space-ships are different colors. That's encouraging - maybe I can communicate with them. The sun is rising over the mountains, and the alien ships are rising too, becoming more colorful. Some of them are really pretty. Good grief - they're balloons! The field is filled with dozens of them lifting into the sky. I will discover later that I've watched the start of the Annual Balloon Festival, which takes off from the field behind my trailer.

"The neighbors are talking," Sophia tells me, "They think the festival should get out of our field."

I do, too. The neighbors are right - but not always. I swam a lot that week, the Balloon Festival left, and I figured it was time for me to do the same. Winter was moving in with its black skies and blue cold. Mornings were layered with snow, the horses put up, and the air smelt of burning wood. The shutters of Ranchos de Taos were closing. It was time to load up the Lincoln and head back to Portland, a painter less lonely - but a drug lord? Not this year.

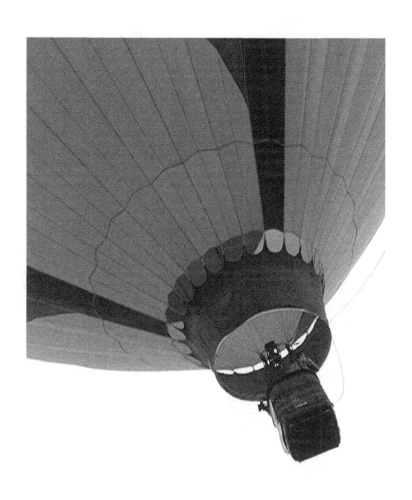

ESSE QUAM VIDERI

"Your clay pot's been fired. You can come pick it up."

"How did it turn out?"

"It looks good," Tom says.

I've come to North Carolina to teach English, and don't know anybody, so I figure I'll take a clay workshop and maybe meet some people, but I find myself sitting alone, strangling a scoop of mud. My quarrel with the clay finally produces a squatting troll. Tom thought it might make a cookie jar. Pleased, I paint it bright colors and leave it with Tom to be fired.

"I'm here for my cookie jar," I tell Tom, who appears to be holding up a loaf of burned bread.

"You're looking at it."

"What happened to the *color*?"

"It changes in the firing."

Tom hands me the dreadful lump and says, "The color looks good."

"*What* color?"

I take the thing and go home.

That's how I met Tom, and I carried that ball of clay with me for years, telling people it was a meteorite. It had come from far away, as had Tom, who'd come from Minnesota to North Carolina to teach ceramics. Gypsy, a weaver in Stokes County, owned a piece of a mountain and gave Tom an acre on which to build a house and settle, weaving him right into the land. The house still sits, fifty years later, in the woods off Piney Mountain Road. Back then it had no plumbing or electricity but it had a sauna and tall pines to keep the sky up.

The first time I drove out to Walnut Cove with Tom, he stopped his truck on an empty stretch of road.

"What're we stopping for," I asked.

"There's a turtle in the road."

Where I come from people don't stop for turtles.

Where I *came* from was New York City, and why I was here, with Tom, in his truck, was that I needed a job. It seemed at the end of the school year, budget concerns called for cutting out a teacher, and it was me. A boarding school in North Carolina was looking for teachers to work with teen-age boys who had learning problems, and I got hired for the summer. So I pulled out of New York City and drove south, my worn-out roots riding with me. My marriage hadn't worked. My foray into dance hadn't worked. And in the end, I hadn't worked. In the rearview mirror the last four years dissolved away into what hadn't happened. Done.

New Jersey, Washington, Virginia, North Carolina, East Fifth Street. Teacher, you're here. My stomach hurt as I pulled into the school parking lot. Then there occurred one of those incandescent moments that seem to come from nowhere and change everything. A boy's thin voice called out, "Reckon that's him!" and I knew that North Carolina would be more than a summer in my life.

Room and board came with the job and, after dropping off my stuff, I went to meet the chairman of the English Department.

"Hello."

"Hello. I'm Dr. Nickels."

"Hello."

"You're different from what we were expecting."

That didn't take long. Here comes a budget crisis.

"How so?" I try.

"Well, more - different." Dr. Nickels smiles.

Hello.

Different. Well, we don't have turtles walking around in New York City but Hazel Nickels could probably tell from looking at me that I wouldn't know a turtle if it climbed up my leg. I recalled that talk with Tom then as we sat in his truck near clay fields and umber-colored barns, and waited for that turtle to finish walking.

"We call them terrapins," Tom said.

In time, I begin to feel the easy coming and going of others as I grow a new life. Summer went beyond itself into another year, and then another, and another. Like the turtle, time was in no hurry.

"Soft rain," Gypsy said, "It bends the leaves back."

She told us that life goes quickly, and I saw John watch her look off into the pines. Susan said that the Bay tree had grown, and that Gypsy knew she was an old woman.

We are like old times in Gypsy's country. Walking in the night. All of us, Tom, Susan, John, Wanda, Gypsy and me. Quiet until the teapot calls us to the kitchen, then back to being quiet again. The clouds are changing - that was the first I noticed it. Mornings are cold. September comes like June came - a caress, a sense of it. Wanda gave me a yellow mountain to paint, and when we hugged one another there was a kind of holding on before another time began.

Susan said, "The horses got out last night so I went out to put them up. Then I sat late on the back porch to watch the wind blow the clouds across the moon."

I said I thought the moon held a lot of water.

"Like March," she whispered.

I enter my classroom, and two boys are fighting so I climb up on top of a desk, and sit there watching. Then, while they continue to fight, I put a jazz record on the phonograph I've set up earlier in the day, and sit there reading a <u>Classics Illustrated</u>. The boys keep fighting but the sounds in the room are changing. I remain absorbed in the comic book but my ears are watching - and waiting.

"Hey, man, cool it!"

"Wuz he readin' theah?"

"Whah ain't he stoppin the faht?"

Some finger popping to the music. Less scuffling. I keep reading the comic. Silence. I look up at an army of puzzled eyes.

"Finish your fight. I want to finish my comic."

"Whudcha readin?"

The circle of eyes move in. I feel a flush of excitement. A boy sticks his head under the cover of the book.

"He readin' <u>The Invisible Man</u>."

"Oh I know thet stoery !"

"Yeah, ah saw thet movie!"

I say, "This is a different story. You probably don't know it."

"Oh yeah?"

"Yeah," I answer.

"Ah *know* thet stoery."

From somewhere, "What's it about, Charlie?"

The eyes face Charlie.

"It's about this gah who..."

and he proceeds with his telling until,

"No, it wuz 'iz waf..."

and,

"He din't have no waf..."

and,

"Hey, y'all forgot the ol' lady..."

"Uh uh..."

And the air explodes with hands.

Then there was Susan in her party dress and high-heeled shoes. She didn't look like any teacher I ever had. But then again, neither did I.

"There's a lot of noise in my classroom," I told her.

"If you listen to these boys," she said, "they'll tell you what to do."

"How do you know that?"

"Because everything's like that," she answered and followed her red shoes down the hall, out of the building and into her truck.

Susan was right about a lot of things. There are, hanging on Susan's wall, two posters:

BLOOM WHERE YOU ARE PLANTED

IF THERE IS NO WIND - ROW

And, pasted on a piece of white muslin, a page of faded wide-lined school paper on which is carefully printed in pencil:

GOD BLESS MISS THOMAS

Pinned to the inside of the door is a card with yellow flowers painted around the edges:

In appreciation.

Our lives are surely much richer

since we have come to know you.

And a poem written by Susan, Sunday morning, November 16, 1975:

Those withering ones who've bloomed their days away,

Look at them nodding and blowing

without understanding,

Dryly, softly, gently

sowing their life on the wind.

And a postcard from John, PM Nov., 1964, with a poem by
S.T.Coleridge:

> *"If a man could pass through Paradise in a dream,*
>
> *and have a flower presented to him as a pledge*
>
> *that his soul had really been there, and if he*
>
> *found that flower in his hand when he awoke -*
>
> *Ay! and what then?"*

"HEY, MR. CAT!"

Their energy is released - and I go for it.

"I should have brought that great record I have of
this story but I guess since we're an English class I should
pass out some books now."

"OH NO!"

"Ah cain't read."

"Wheah thet record at?"

"We want to heah thet record."

"It might be in my office, but I can't walk out of here. You'll tear the room up."

"NO WE WON'T!"

"Get thet record, Mr. Cat."

I look at the boys. The boys look back at me.

"How many want to hear that record?" I ask.

Again, the room explodes with hands.

"OK."

I get the record and two kerosene lamps.

"Let's push the desks out of the way and spread out on the floor. Fast - we don't have much time left."

"We'll skip ouah next class."

"You'll skip out the door when the bell rings. You - pull down the shades, please. Charlie, get the lights, will ya?"

There we sat in a quiet circle, in darkness.

"You, will you please light the kerosene lamps?"

"Now, close your eyes and imagine you're alone in an old empty house way out in the country. And it's late at night and there's a big storm outside. If anyone is too scared, he can leave now."

"OK."

"How long will it take for that turtle to get where it's going?" I asked Tom.

"Until it gets there," he laughed.

So we sat in the truck and looked at the fields and I saw how red they were.

"Red clay," Tom said. "It grows things."

And I looked at his strong hands.

This morning my classroom is transformed into a raging thunderstorm. I watch the boys, their eyes shining like fireflies in the dark. The defiance is gone from their faces. I like them. The period is about to end so I stop at a suspenseful point in the story.

"Oh no! Don't stop!"

"Time to go. I'll see you tomorrow morning at eight sharp!"

"We'll stay."

"You'll go."

I leave the lights out and the lamps burning. And my disgruntled class stumbles out into the hallway, their complaints muted by the sounds of thunder. No fighting in here today. The following morning, everyone was on the floor waiting at 7:45 when I arrived for class. The lights were out - and so were matches waiting to light the lamps.

The wind was warm the night Tom went to see Gypsy at the hospital. They talked about the weather and the craft fair. Gypsy told Tom to keep a watch on everyone, mostly Susan - and it was time to go.

The nurse said, "Shall I close the window for you, Mrs. Hollingsworth?"

"Don't bother to do that," Gypsy answered, "I'll be going spiriting tonight."

Off of Piney Mountain Road, about a quarter of a mile through the woods, is a two acre clearing which is Susan's piece of land. On it stands a small stable which housed the horse the Susan bought from a woman in Virginia and which turned out to be lame. The horse's leg had been shot full of cortisone or something which made it seem to be ok and when Susan got the horse home the stuff wore off and it limped. Susan didn't take the horse back because she didn't want to hurt the woman's feelings and figured if she hadn't bought it somebody else would have or it would have been shot. Later, in a bad trade she lost the horse and wound up with nothing. The stable is empty and the door lies open banging against the building in the wind.

Susan Thomas was once my wildly restless red-haired friend. She loved her green satin dress, her black stockings and her cadmium red shoes, as did I. Gypsy gave Susan Thomas Young a small meadow on which to build a house and raise her baby. The one-room house looks down through still trees onto a dark pond. It is painted red and

190

has a tin roof for listening to the rain. It has a portable heater next to a crib, a painting of a tall tree in orange foliage on a plywood divider between the toilet and the washer and dryer, bowls of dusty field flowers, a saddle, a radio, a photograph of a red-haired baby, a panda bear, a double bed with one pillow, a Sweet Sixteen Donuts bag with three left and a ten pound bag of Purina Cat Chow.

When I left Walnut Cove it was raining. John was rubbing a leaf in his hands, and there was a fly in the room. Gypsy said, "Well come and stay." As I drove away I watched their arms in the rearview mirror turn to waving grass. During the night the car and I broke down in Virginia, on 85 North. I pulled off the road, put a sign on the window, HELP, curled up with the thunder of trucks, and waited.

The boys I came to teach are grown up now, as are their sons and daughters. Tom has electricity, and Susan's baby is a woman. I wonder how many of us Gypsy wove into her land so that we might grow. North Carolina took up my roots, and has fed my heart for fifty years now. The terrapin's still walking across the road. And I'm still waiting on it.

EPILOGUE

"What is made by time, time respects it." - *Henri Cartier-Bresson*

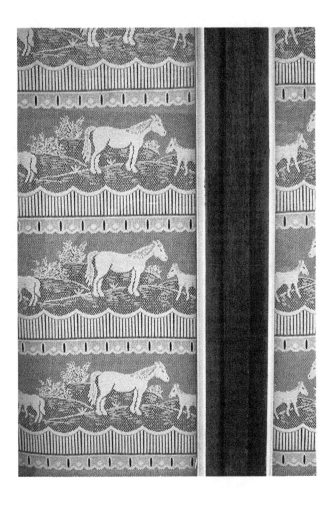

THE CONTRACT

"Inanimate things don't talk," she said to me. "You may feel like the studio is talking to you but it can't talk."

"It does talk," I replied.

When I was growing up, my grandmother took me to an art class for children, held at the Art Museum. I expect she was sorry she took me there when I walked out with a clay sculpture of a naked woman.

"What are *those?*" Gram asked, pointing to a pair of uncertain cones.

"That's what they looked like."

"Are *those* her bosoms!" she cried, and we didn't go back to that class.

But we went to others. I think my Russian grandmother believed that exposure to art would give me some polish - so we ran around and took classes. When I resisted, Gram bought me stuff like neon hot socks. Then I went - and wound up liking art more than Gram did. *Polish* was part of what Gram valued - but not the *whole* part. In time, one had to make a living but one didn't have to make art. So in time I went out *to make a living*. But I thought about art all the time.

For years, I carried around a small sketchbook and, when making a living got to me, I drew in it – and from it. Sketching in public places could draw "You're a *good* artist!" out of somebody, ratcheting up my self-esteem. Making a drawing became a kind of antidote to making a living. Then, during a break between jobs, I started to paint full time. My initial euphoria eventually settled as long days and nights in the studio, and I sensed a show-down ripening. One night while looking at a collection of my paintings pinned on the dining room wall, it happened. "These are *good*," I said aloud. It was the first time I'd expressed belief in my work, rather than seeking it from others.

"You're looking good but I'm bushed! What do you want from me?"

And that wall comes back with, "I *want your life*."

"But I don't *do life*. Never have."

"Okay."

"Maybe we can work something out."

"Don't think so. I don't bargain. That's my price."

"Sorry, no deal."

I figured I could still pop off a sketch in a restaurant, pull *"That's good!"* out of somebody, and walk out feeling like somebody myself. Painting was wanting to take over my life in ways I hadn't expected.

My romantic delusions about *colorful can-cans at The Moulin Rouge in Paris* went out the window; *my* can-can was with a dining room wall in Durham, Oregon.

"No go," I repeated. "I'll just keep sketching."

"No problem. Give me *that* - and I'll give it back to you."

"Give me back *what?*"

"How about adolescence forever? I'll give you folks in restaurants who, like your grandmother, will settle for less from you. That's fine with me - but if you want to grow it will cost you your life."

"I'll settle for arrested development."

"Have a nice life."

That did it - I stopped painting! *The end!* For months I kind of *bubbled* about. It was a relief: no paintings developing in my head; no waking up at night; no failures to get past; no tension - *no nothing*. Then pop! - a bubble burst. Pop! Pop! Pop! Plop! - I went *flat*. Worse - performing in restaurants didn't work anymore. I had no *life*, so I went back to talk to the wall.

"All right - you win. I'll give you my life but I think it's a mirage."

"You're on," the wall replied, "and, by the way, I'm giving you back something - a *real* life. *You* win."

The dining room turned the tables on me that night, something my grandmother never did. *The wall* knew it was time to make a call - settle up, choose, and get on with it. So don't tell me that inanimate objects don't talk! Sometimes, I guess, it just takes them some time.